MENSA
PUBLICATIONS

MATH GAMES
FOR
KIDS

HAROLD GALE &
CAROLYN SKITT

P Prima Publishing
3875 Atherton Road
Rocklin, CA 95765
(916) 632 4400

THIS IS A CARLTON BOOK

Text and puzzles copyright © Mensa Publications 1994
Design and artwork copyright © Carlton Books Limited 1994

Prima Publishing, Rocklin, CA 95765

Printed and bound in Italy

96 95 94 93 10 9 8 7 6 5 4 3 2 1

Library of Congress Cataloging-in-Publication Data
is available on request

ISBN 1-55958-592-7

MENSA
PUBLICATIONS

MATH GAMES
FOR
KIDS

★ INTRODUCTION ★

We welcome you to the world of numbers. This book has been specially written for you by Carolyn Skitt and myself. The puzzles are divided into six different levels of difficulty, starting from Level A which is quite easy, to Level F which is mind-numbing!

In this book you will meet dinosaurs, zap spaceships and count coins from the distant planet of Venox. In fact, you'll have all sorts of weird and wonderful adventures. There are unusual boxes to be made, animals to trace through and flags with a difference. These puzzles, along with many, many others, will give you hours of pleasure – and that's not all. The more you use your brain the sharper it will become and so, having wandered through the easier sections, you will come up against the more difficult sections.

But how difficult are they? You will probably find them a lot easier after doing the earlier sections than they look at first sight, because you will already have had the practice. And think how pleased with yourself you'll be when you can solve puzzles that you thought were impossible.

Harold Gale,
Executive Director of British Mensa

★ MENSA MINI IQ TEST ★

Take 10 minutes only to complete the test.

1 If a circle is one how many is an octagon?

2 There are 1,200 elephants in a herd. Some have pink and blue stripes, some are all pink and some are all blue. Of these one third are pure pink. Is it true that 400 elephants are definitely blue?

3 Which vowel comes midway between J and T?

4 Which number comes next in this series of numbers?

1 2 3 5 7 11 13 ?

5 Which letter comes next in this series of letters?

B A C B D C E D F ?

6 Which of these is the odd one out?

CAT DOG HAMSTER RABBIT ELK

7 Which word can be added to the end of GRASS and the beginning of SCAPE to form two other English words?

8 The zoo has two lions. A lion eats three pounds of meat each day. A lioness eats two pounds of meat each day and a lion cub eats one pound of meat. The delivery for today is two pounds of meat and that is all the meat available for the zoo. Must any or both of the lions go hungry?

9 If six minus one is worth nine and seven minus five is worth one. How much is six plus ten worth?

10 Which word of four letters can be added to the front of the following words to create other English words?

CARD BOX CODE BAG HASTE

ANSWERS

1 8.
2 No.
3 O.
4 17. (They are all prime numbers.)
5 E.
6 Elk.
7 Land.
8 No, they could be lion cubs.
9 9. Value of Roman numerals in words, if any, either subtracted or added.
10 Post.

Score	Comment	Possible IQ
10	Excellent	160
9	Very Good Indeed	155
8	Mensa Level	148
7	Good	130
6	Above Average	115
5	Average	100
4	Below Average	90
3	Well Below Average	80
2	Poor	65
1	Very Poor Indeed	50

NOW TRY THIS ONE:
Your watch was correct at midnight but then began to gain two and a half minutes every hour. It stopped two hours ago showing quarter past six in the morning. What should the watch be showing?

If you think you have the correct answer send it to Mensa on a postcard or the back of an envelope and you will receive a certificate of merit, along with Mensa details. The address to reply to is:
MENSA HOUSE, ST JOHN'S SQUARE, WOLVERHAMPTON WV2 1AH, ENGLAND.

EASY DOES IT

PUZZLE 1

Using the numbers shown how many different ways are there to add three numbers together to make a total of 8? A number can be used more than once, but a group cannot be repeated in a different order?

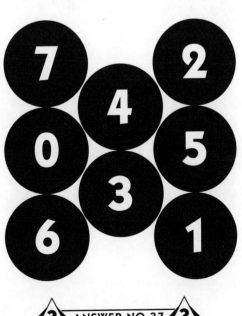

ANSWER NO.37

PUZZLE 2

Move up or across from the bottom left-hand 1 to the top right-hand 1. Collect nine numbers and add them together. What is the highest you can score?

ANSWER NO.169

PUZZLE 3

Join together the dots using odd numbers only.
Start at the lowest and discover the object. What is it?

ANSWER NO.122

EASY DOES IT

A

PUZZLE 4

Place in the middle box a number larger than 1.
If the number is the correct one, all the other numbers can be divided
by it without leaving any remainder. What is the number?

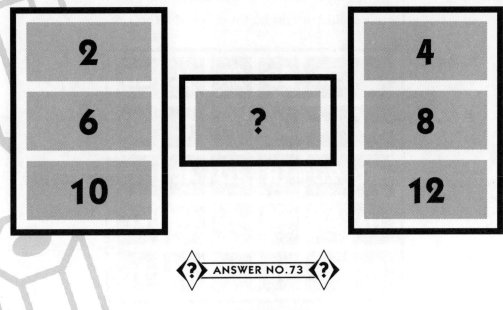

ANSWER NO.73

PUZZLE 5

Each sector of the circle follows a pattern.
What number should replace the question mark?

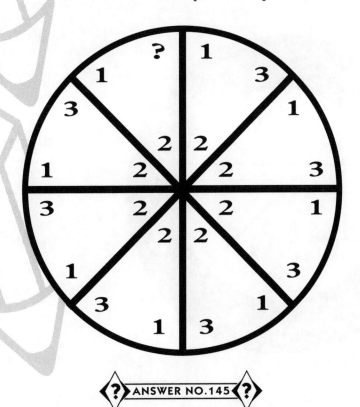

ANSWER NO.145

PUZZLE 6

Here is an unusual safe. Each of the buttons must be pressed only once in the correct order to open it. The last button is marked F. The number of moves and the direction is marked on each button. Thus 1U would mean one move up, whilst 1L would mean one move to the left. Which button is the first you must press? Here's a clue: it can be found on the top row.

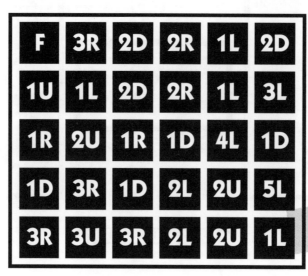

F	3R	2D	2R	1L	2D
1U	1L	2D	2R	1L	3L
1R	2U	1R	1D	4L	1D
1D	3R	1D	2L	2U	5L
3R	3U	3R	2L	2U	1L

ANSWER NO.26

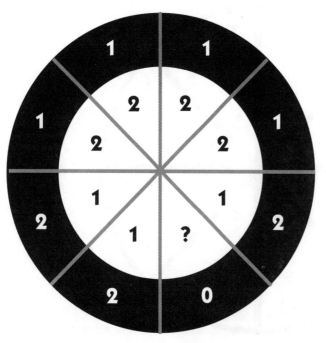

PUZZLE 7

Each slice of this cake adds up to the same number. What number should replace the question mark?

ANSWER NO.13

PUZZLE 8

Copy out these shapes carefully and rearrange them to form a number. What is it?

❮?❯ ANSWER NO.196 ❮?❯

PUZZLE 9

If you look carefully you should see why the numbers are written as they are.
What number should replace the question mark?

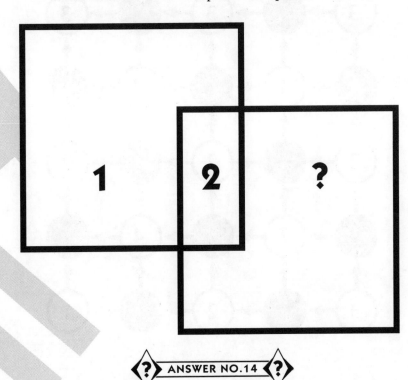

❮?❯ ANSWER NO.14 ❮?❯

PUZZLE 10

Look at the pattern of numbers in the diagram.
What number should replace the question mark?

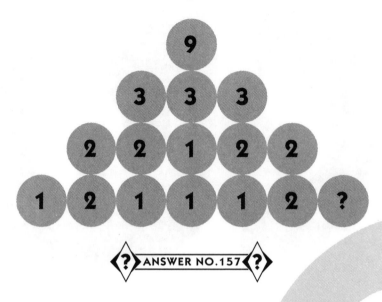

ANSWER NO.157

PUZZLE 11

Move from the bottom left-hand 3 to the top right-hand 3 adding together
all five numbers. Each black circle is worth 1 and this should be added to your
total each time you meet one. What is the highest total you can find?

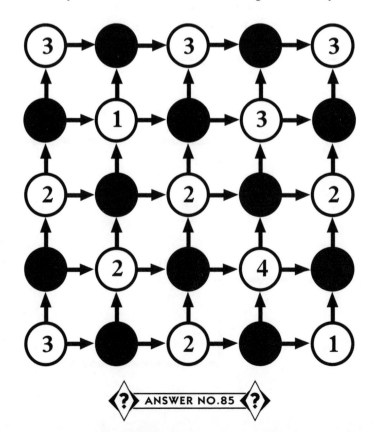

ANSWER NO.85

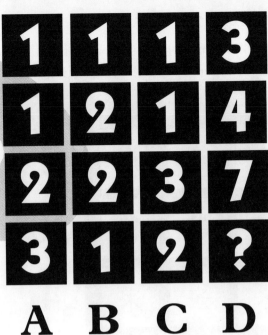

A	B	C	D
1	1	1	3
1	2	1	4
2	2	3	7
3	1	2	?

PUZZLE 12

The numbers in column D are linked in some way to those in A, B and C. What number should replace the question mark?

ANSWER NO.133

PUZZLE 13

Start at the A and move to B passing through various parts of the rhinoceros. There is a number in each part and these must be added together. What is the lowest number you can total?

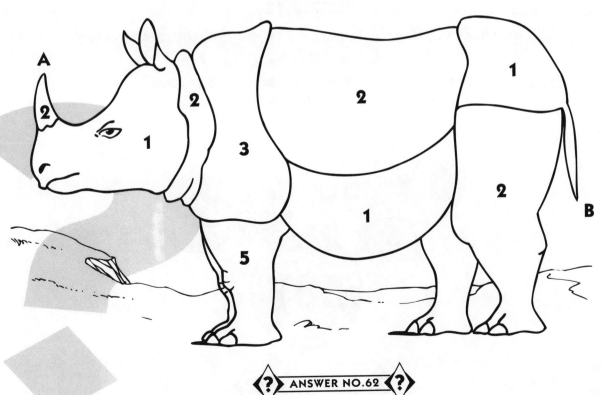

ANSWER NO.62

LEVEL A

PUZZLE 14

Each symbol is worth a number. The total of the symbols can be found alongside each row. What number should replace the question mark?

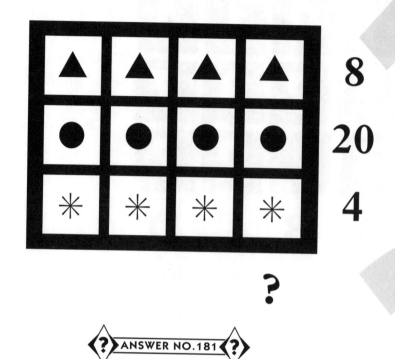

8

20

4

?

ANSWER NO.181

PUZZLE 15

On the planet Venox the coins used are 1V, 2V, 5V, 10V, 20V and 50V.
A Venoxian has 85V in his squiggly bank.
He has the same number of three kinds of coin.
How many of each are there and what are they?

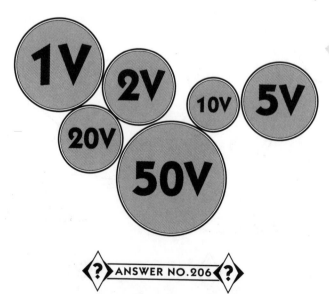

ANSWER NO.206

PUZZLE 16

What is the lowest number of lines needed to divide the camel so that you can find the numbers 1, 2 and 3 in each selection?

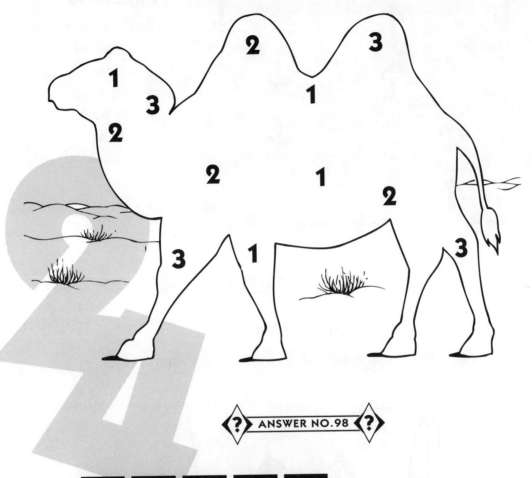

❓ ANSWER NO.98 ❓

PUZZLE 17

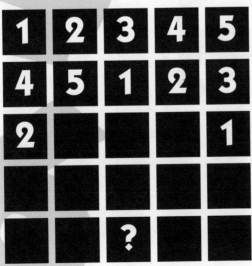

Fill up this square with the numbers 1 to 5 so that no row, column or diagonal line of five squares uses the same number more than once. What number should replace the question mark?

❓ ANSWER NO.217 ❓

LEVEL A

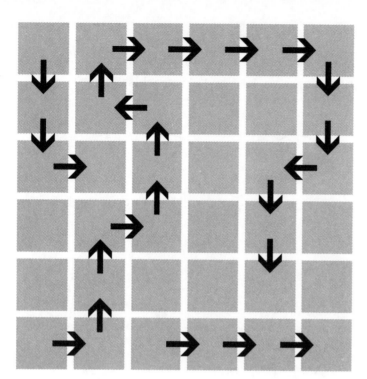

PUZZLE 18

Follow the arrows
and find the
longest
possible route.
How many
boxes have
been entered?

ANSWER NO.109

PUZZLE 19

The symbol on the flag will give a number. What is it?

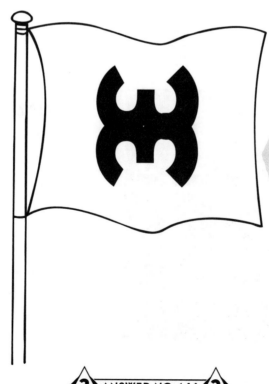

ANSWER NO.146

PUZZLE 20

Start at the middle 3 and move from circle to touching circle.
Collect three numbers and add them to the 3.
How many different routes are there to make a total of 8?

? ANSWER NO.25 ?

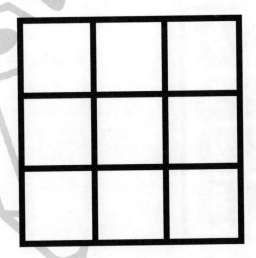

PUZZLE 21

How many squares
of any size can
you find in
this diagram?

? ANSWER NO.1 ?

PUZZLE 22

The first set of scales balance.
How many A's will make the second set balance?

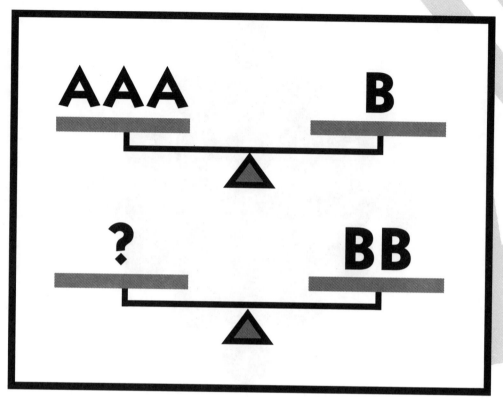

ANSWER NO.121

PUZZLE 23

Divide up the box
using four lines so that each
shape adds up to the same.
How is this done?

ANSWER NO.182

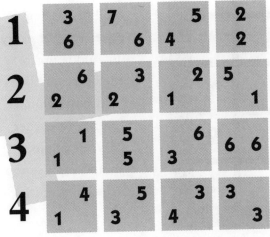

A B C D

	A	B	C	D
1	3 6	7 6	5 4	2 2
2	6 2	3 2	2 1	5 1
3	1 1	5 5	6 3	6 6
4	4 1	5 3	3 4	3 3

PUZZLE 24

Which squares contain the same numbers?

? ANSWER NO.134 ?

PUZZLE 25

Turn the number shown on the calculator into 32 by pressing two buttons only. What are they?

? ANSWER NO.86 ?

LEVEL A

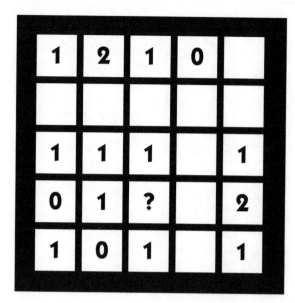

1	2	1	0	
1	1	1		1
0	1	?		2
1	0	1		1

PUZZLE 26

Fill in the empty boxes so that every line adds up to 5, including the lines that go from corner to corner. What number should replace the question mark?

ANSWER NO.61

PUZZLE 27

Copy out these shapes carefully and rearrange them to form a number. What is it?

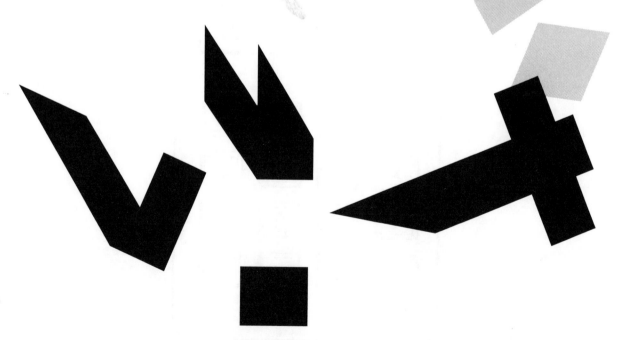

ANSWER NO.194

PUZZLE 28

Which number should be placed in the triangle to continue the series?

ANSWER NO.38

PUZZLE 29

Here is a series of numbers.
Which number should replace the question mark?

ANSWER NO.193

PUZZLE 30

Replace each question mark with either plus, minus, multiply or divide.
Each sign can be used more than once. When the correct ones have been used
the sum will be completed. What are the signs?

ANSWER NO.97

LEVEL A

PUZZLE 31

Which of these pictures is not of the same box?

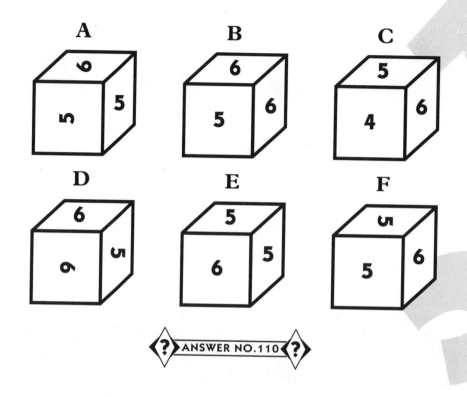

A **B** **C**

D **E** **F**

ANSWER NO.110

PUZZLE 32

How many 3's can be found in this Pterodactyl?

ANSWER NO.158

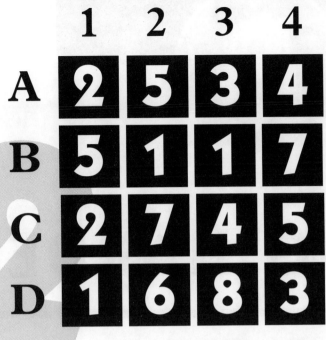

	1	2	3	4
A	2	5	3	4
B	5	1	1	7
C	2	7	4	5
D	1	6	8	3

PUZZLE 33

Find the correct six numbers to put in the frame. There are two choices for each square, for example 1A would give the number 2. When the correct numbers have been found an easy series will appear. What is the series?

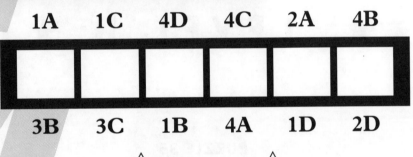

1A	1C	4D	4C	2A	4B
3B	3C	1B	4A	1D	2D

◇⟨?⟩ ANSWER NO.205 ⟨?⟩◇

LEVEL A

1	12	2
3	36	6
4	42	2
5	55	5
7	78	?

PUZZLE 34

The numbers in the middle section have some connection with those down the sides. Find out what it is and tell us what should replace the question mark?

◇⟨?⟩ ANSWER NO.2 ⟨?⟩◇

GETTING HARDER

★ LEVEL B ★

PUZZLE 35

The numbers in the middle section have some connection with those down the sides.
Find out what it is and tell us what should replace the question mark?

3	23	2
1	61	6
7	47	4
5	35	3
9	?	1

◆? ANSWER NO.4 ?◆

PUZZLE 36

Which number should be placed in the triangle to continue the series?

? ANSWER NO.40 ?

PUZZLE 37

Zap the spaceship by making its number a round one. Take off either 11, 13, 19, 21 or 25 to do this. Which number ought you to use?

LEVEL B

? ANSWER NO.76 ?

PUZZLE 38

Move up or across from the bottom left-hand 2 to the top right-hand 1.
Collect nine numbers and add them together. What is the highest you can score?

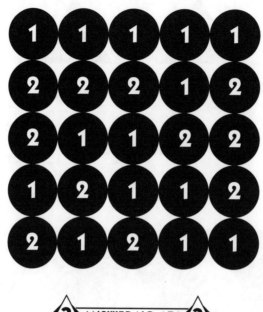

ANSWER NO.171

PUZZLE 39

Start at any corner and follow the lines. Add up the first four numbers you meet
and then add on the corner number. What is the lowest you can score?

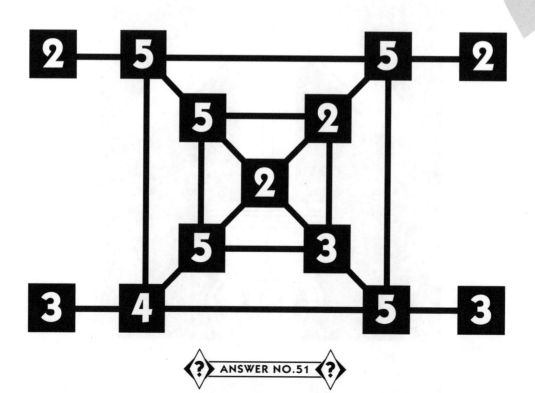

ANSWER NO.51

PUZZLE 40

Place in the middle box a number larger than 1.
If the number is the correct one, all the other numbers can be divided
by it without leaving any remainder. What is the number?

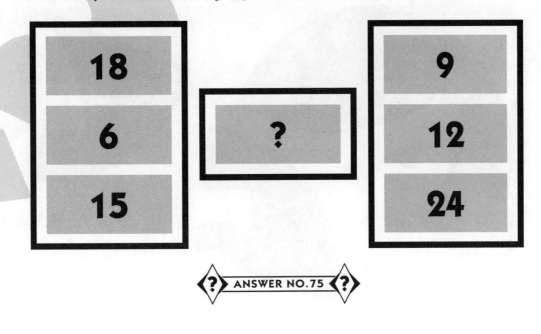

ANSWER NO.75

PUZZLE 41

Each sector of the circle follows a pattern.
What number should replace the question mark?

ANSWER NO.147

PUZZLE 42

Copy the cake slices out carefully and rearrange them to find the birthday.
How old was the birthday boy?

? ANSWER NO.172 **?**

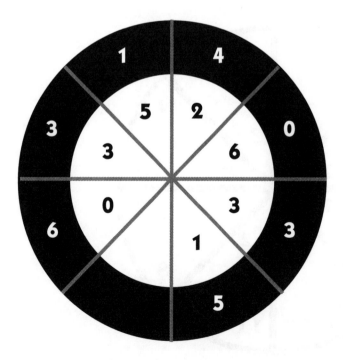

PUZZLE 43

Each slice of this cake adds
up to the same number.
All the numbers going
round the cake total 24.
Which two numbers should
appear on the blank slice?

? ANSWER NO.15 **?**

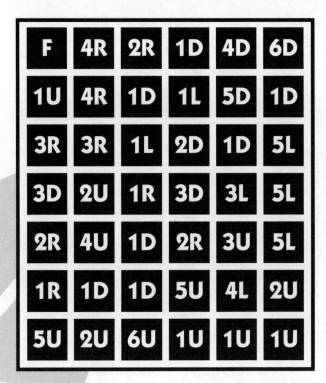

F	4R	2R	1D	4D	6D
1U	4R	1D	1L	5D	1D
3R	3R	1L	2D	1D	5L
3D	2U	1R	3D	3L	5L
2R	4U	1D	2R	3U	5L
1R	1D	1D	5U	4L	2U
5U	2U	6U	1U	1U	1U

PUZZLE 44

Here is an unusual safe. Each of the buttons must be pressed only once in the correct order to open it. The last button is marked F. The number of moves and the direction is marked on each button. Thus 1U would mean one move up, whilst 1L would mean one move to the left. Which button is the first you must press? Here's a clue: it can be found on the middle row.

ANSWER NO.28

PUZZLE 45

If you look carefully you should see why the numbers are written as they are. What number should replace the question mark?

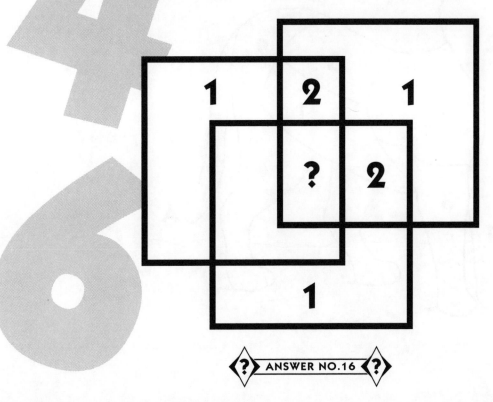

ANSWER NO.16

LEVEL B

PUZZLE 46

Look at the pattern of numbers in the diagram.
What number should replace the question mark?

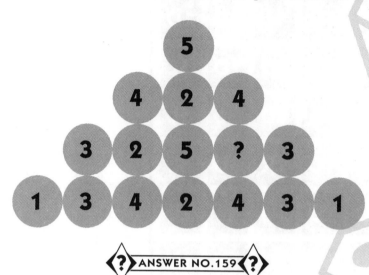

ANSWER NO.159

PUZZLE 47

Start at the A and move to B passing through the various parts of the cat.
There is a number in each part and these must be added together.
What is the lowest number you can total?

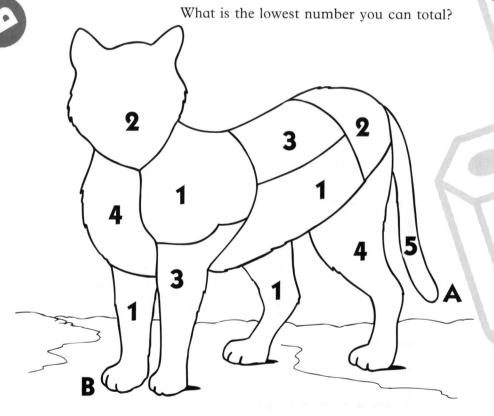

ANSWER NO.64

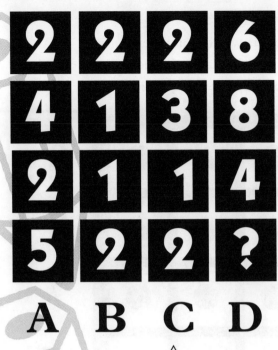

The numbers in column D are linked in some way to those in A, B and C. What number should replace the question mark?

A B C D

ANSWER NO.135

PUZZLE 49

Move from the bottom left-hand 5 to the top right-hand 2 adding together all five numbers. Each black circle is worth 2 and this should be added to your total each time you meet one. What is the highest total you can find?

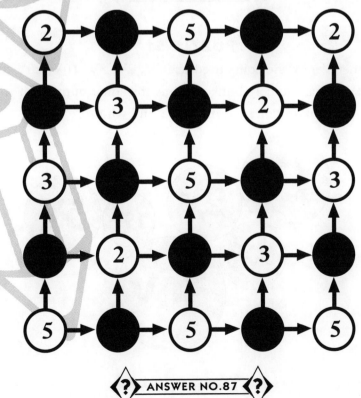

ANSWER NO.87

LEVEL B

B

PUZZLE 50

Each symbol is worth a number.

The total of the symbols can be found alongside each row and column.

What number should replace the question mark?

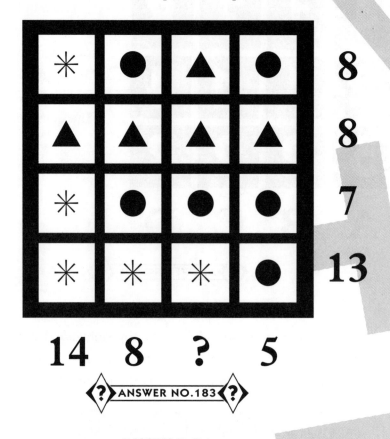

ANSWER NO.183

PUZZLE 51

On the planet Venox the coins used are 1V, 2V, 5V, 10V, 20V and 50V.

A Venoxian has 374V in his squiggly bank. He has the same number of three kinds of coin.

How many of each are there and what are they?

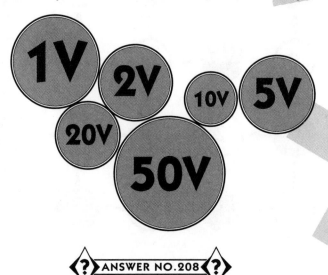

ANSWER NO.208

PUZZLE 52

What is the lowest number of lines needed to divide the elephant so that you can find the numbers 1, 2, 3 and 4 in each section?

 ANSWER NO.100

PUZZLE 53

Here is a series of numbers. Which number should replace the question mark?

| 4 | 8 | 12 | 16 | 20 | 24 | ? |

ANSWER NO.195

PUZZLE 54

Replace each question mark with either plus, minus, multiply or divide. Each sign can be used more than once. When the correct ones have been used the sum will be completed. What are the signs?

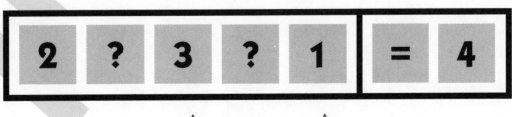

| 2 | ? | 3 | ? | 1 | = | 4 |

ANSWER NO.99

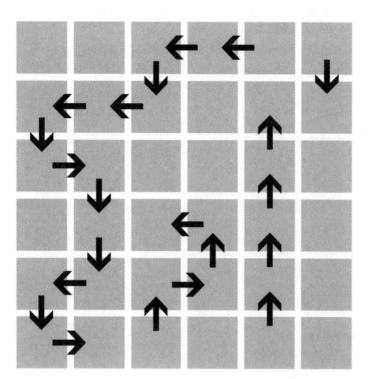

PUZZLE 55

Follow the arrows and find
the longest possible route.
How many boxes have
been entered?

ANSWER NO.111

PUZZLE 56

The symbol on the flag will give a number. What is it?

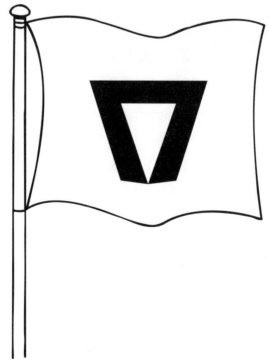

ANSWER NO.148

PUZZLE 57

Start at the middle 1 and move from circle to touching circle.

Collect three numbers and add them to the 1.

How many different routes are there to make a total of 10?

? ANSWER NO.27 ?

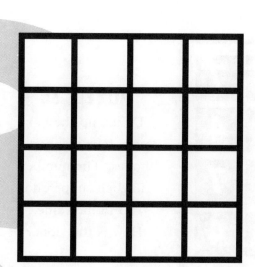

PUZZLE 58

How many squares
of any size can
you find in
this diagram?

? ANSWER NO.3 ?

PUZZLE 59

Scales 1 and 2 are in perfect balance.
How many A's are needed to balance the third set?

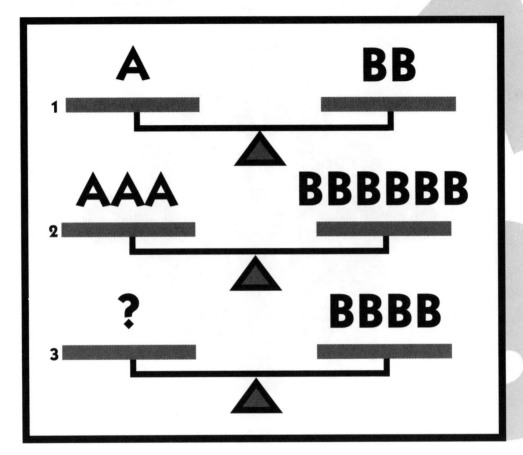

ANSWER NO.123

PUZZLE 60

Divide up the box into four identical shapes. The numbers in each shape add up to the same. How is this done?

ANSWER NO.184

GETTING HARDER
B

PUZZLE 61

Which squares contain the same numbers?

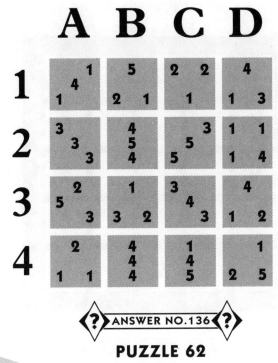

ANSWER NO.136

PUZZLE 62

Which buttons must be used to produce the number on the calculator?

Only three buttons can be used.

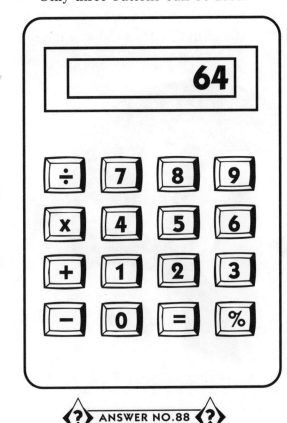

ANSWER NO.88

PUZZLE 63

Fill in the empty boxes so that every line adds up to 10, including the lines that go from corner to corner, using only one number. What is it?

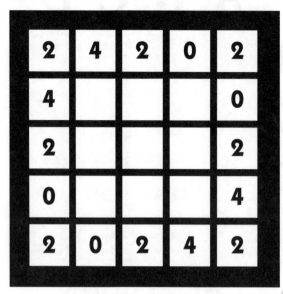

2	4	2	0	2
4				0
2				2
0				4
2	0	2	4	2

◇?◇ ANSWER NO.63 ◇?◇

PUZZLE 64

Copy the cake slices out carefully and rearrange them to find the birthday. How old was the birthday girl?

◇?◇ ANSWER NO.170 ◇?◇

PUZZLE 65

Which of these pictures is not of the same box?

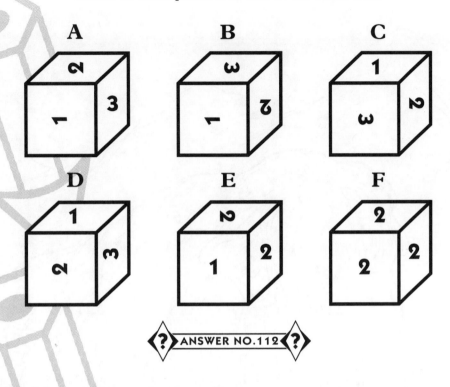

A   B   C

D   E   F

◆?▶ ANSWER NO.112 ◀?◆

PUZZLE 66

Fill up this square with the numbers 1 to 5 so that no row, column
or diagonal line of five squares uses the same number more than once.
What number should replace the question mark?

◆?▶ ANSWER NO.218 ◀?◆

PUZZLE 67

How many 5s can be found in this mammoth?

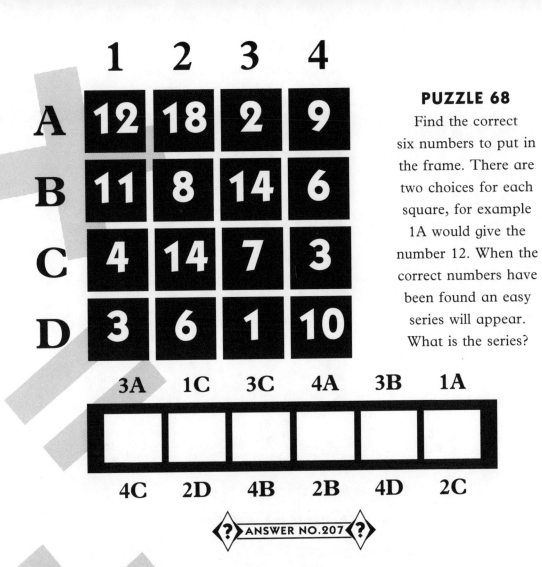

	1	2	3	4
A	12	18	2	9
B	11	8	14	6
C	4	14	7	3
D	3	6	1	10

PUZZLE 68

Find the correct six numbers to put in the frame. There are two choices for each square, for example 1A would give the number 12. When the correct numbers have been found an easy series will appear. What is the series?

3A	1C	3C	4A	3B	1A
4C	2D	4B	2B	4D	2C

ANSWER NO.207

LEVEL B

B

PUZZLE 69

Which of the numbers in the square is the odd one out and why?

4	10	2
14	16	6
7	8	12

ANSWER NO.52

PUZZLE 70

Join together the dots using odd numbers only.
Start at the lowest and discover the object. What is it?

15

23 17

2

14

13

19

25

11 21

18

30

? ANSWER NO.124 **?**

PUZZLE 71

Using the numbers
shown how many
different ways are
there to add three
numbers together to
make a total of 10?
A number can be
used more than once,
but a group cannot
be repeated in a
different order?

5 1
4
7 2
0
8 6

? ANSWER NO.39 **?**

FIENDISH FIGURES

★ LEVEL C ★

PUZZLE 72

The numbers in the middle section have some connection with those down the sides.
Find out what it is and tell us what should replace the question mark?

5	10	5
2	9	7
8	12	4
3	6	3
5	?	6

ANSWER NO.6

PUZZLE 73

Move up or across from the bottom left-hand 3 to the top right-hand 3.
Collect nine numbers and add them together. What is the lowest you can score?

◆?▶ANSWER NO.175 ◆?▶

PUZZLE 74

Start at any corner and follow the lines. Add up the first four numbers you meet
and then add on the corner number. What is the highest you can score?

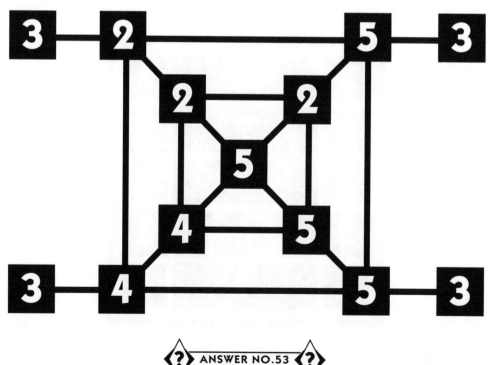

◆?▶ ANSWER NO.53 ◆?▶

PUZZLE 75

Place in the middle box a number larger than 1.
If the number is the correct one, all the other numbers can be divided
by it without leaving any remainder. What is the number?

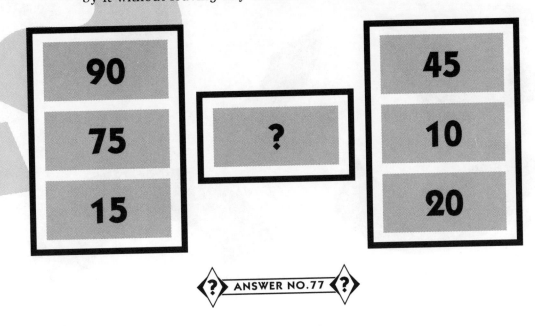

? ANSWER NO.77 ?

PUZZLE 76

Each sector of the circle follows a pattern.
What number should replace the question mark?

? ANSWER NO.149 ?

LEVEL C

PUZZLE 77

Copy out these shapes carefully and rearrange them to form a number.
What is it?

 ANSWER NO.198

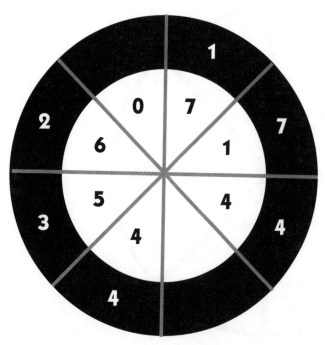

PUZZLE 78

Each slice of this cake adds
up to the same number.
All the numbers going
round the cake total 32.
Which numbers should
appear in the blanks?

 ANSWER NO.17

FIENDISH FIGURES

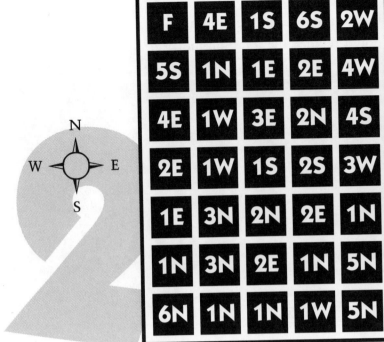

F	4E	1S	6S	2W	6S
5S	1N	1E	2E	4W	2S
4E	1W	3E	2N	4S	2W
2E	1W	1S	2S	3W	2S
1E	3N	2N	2E	1N	1W
1N	3N	2E	1N	5N	5W
6N	1N	1N	1W	5N	4W

PUZZLE 79

Here is an unusual safe. Each of the buttons must be pressed only once in the correct order to open it. The last button is marked F. The number of moves and the direction is marked on each button. Thus 1N would mean one move north, whilst 1W would mean one move to the west. Which button is the first you must press? Here's a clue: it can be found on the middle row.

ANSWER NO.30

PUZZLE 80

If you look carefully you should see why the numbers are written as they are. What number should replace the question mark?

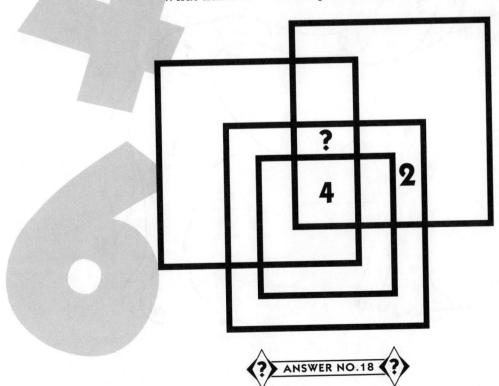

ANSWER NO.18

LEVEL C

PUZZLE 81

Look at each line of numbers in the diagram.
What number should replace the question mark?

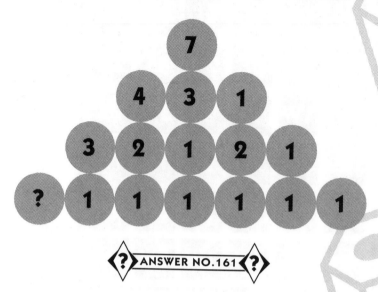

? ANSWER NO.161 ?

PUZZLE 82

Start at the A and move to B passing through the various parts of the horse.
There is a number in each part and these must be added together.
What is the lowest number you can total?

 ? ANSWER NO.66 ?

PUZZLE 83

The numbers in column D are linked in some way to those in A, B and C. What number should replace the question mark?

ANSWER NO.137

PUZZLE 84

Move from the bottom left-hand 4 to the top right-hand 3 adding together all five numbers. Each black circle is worth minus 1 and this should be taken away from your total each time you meet one. What is the highest total you can find?

LEVEL C

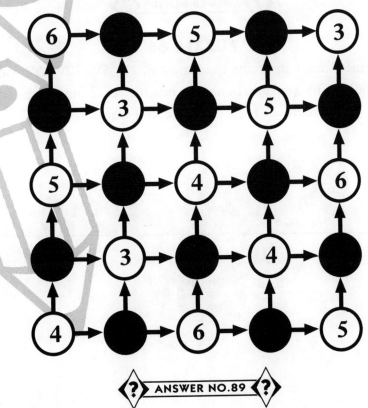

ANSWER NO.89

PUZZLE 85

Each symbol is worth a number. The total of the symbols can be found alongside each row and column. What number should replace the question mark?

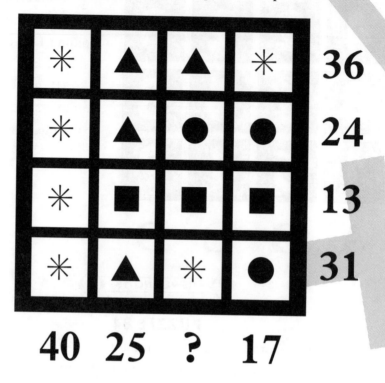

40 25 ? 17

ANSWER NO.185

PUZZLE 86

On the planet Venox the coins used are 1V, 2V, 5V, 10V, 20V and 50V.
A Venoxian has 306V in his squiggly bank. He has the same number of four kinds of coin.
How many of each are there and what are they?

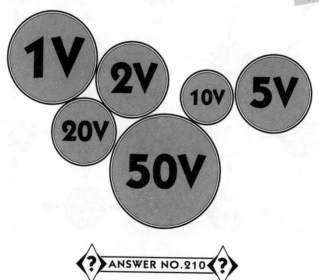

ANSWER NO.210

PUZZLE 87

What is the lowest number of lines needed to divide the rhinoceros so that
you can find the numbers 1, 2, 3, 4 and 5 in each section?

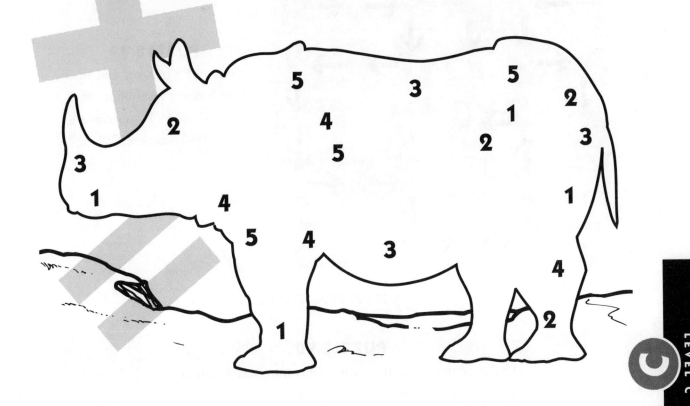

? ANSWER NO.102 ?

PUZZLE 88

Replace each question mark with either plus, minus,
multiply or divide. Each sign can be used more than once.
When the correct ones have been used
the sum will be completed. What are the signs?

| 6 | ? | 3 | ? | 4 | ? | 2 | = | 8 |

? ANSWER NO.101 ?

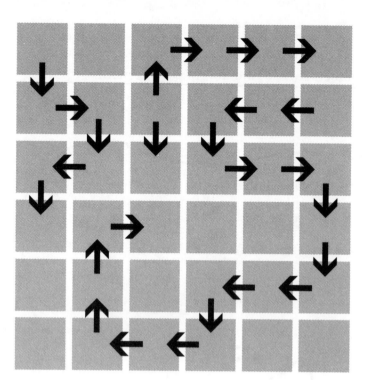

PUZZLE 89

Follow the arrows and find the longest possible route. How many boxes have been entered?

ANSWER NO.113

PUZZLE 90

The symbol on the flag will give a number. What is it?

ANSWER NO.150

PUZZLE 91

Start at the middle 2 and move from circle to touching circle.
Collect three numbers and add them to the 2.
How many different routes are there to make a total of 12?

ANSWER NO.29

PUZZLE 92

Divide up the box
using four lines so
that each shape adds
up to the same.
How is this done?

ANSWER NO.186

PUZZLE 93

Scales 1 and 2 are in perfect balance. If one C is the same as four As, how many As are needed to balance the third set?

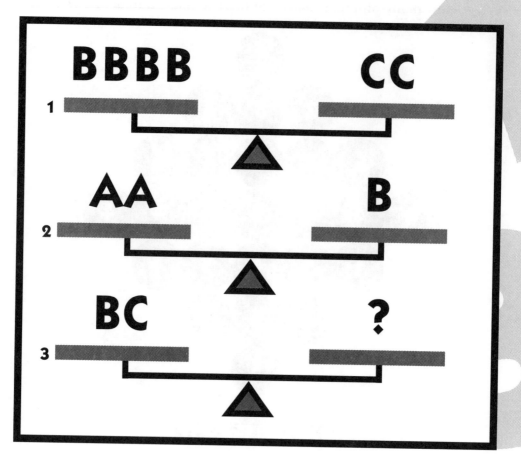

1   BBBB   CC

2   AA   B

3   BC   ?

ANSWER NO.125

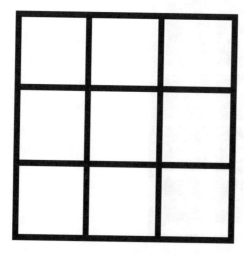

PUZZLE 94

How many rectangles of any size can you find in this diagram? Remember a square is also a rectangle!

ANSWER NO.5

PUZZLE 95

Which squares contain the same numbers?

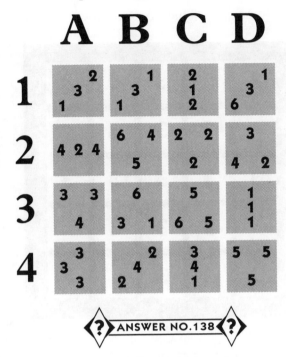

ANSWER NO.138

PUZZLE 96

One two-digit number should be used to divide the one shown on the calculator to get the answer 11. What is the number?

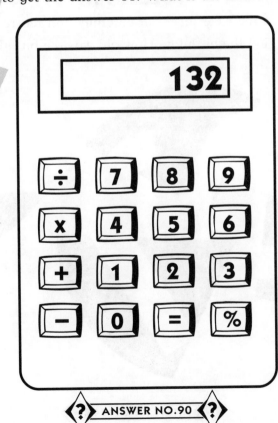

ANSWER NO.90

PUZZLE 97

Fill in the empty boxes so that every line adds up to the same, including the lines that go from corner to corner. Which two numbers will be used to do this?

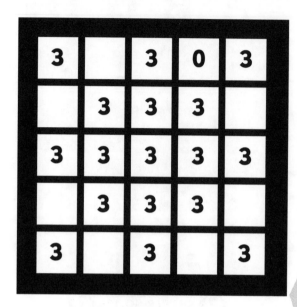

3		3	0	3
	3	3	3	
3	3	3	3	3
	3	3	3	
3		3		3

ANSWER NO.65

PUZZLE 98

Copy the cake slices out carefully and rearrange them to find the birthday. How old was the birthday boy?

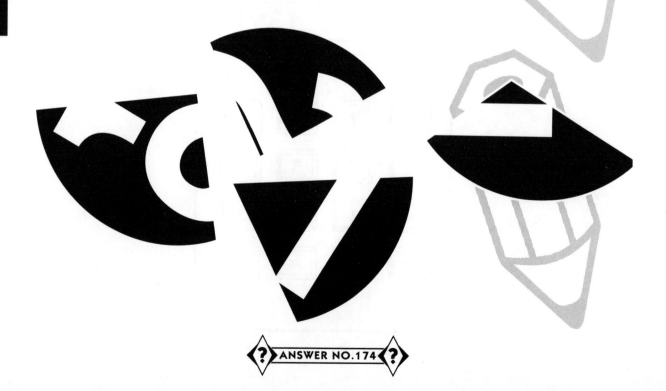

ANSWER NO.174

PUZZLE 99

Which number should replace the question mark to continue the series?

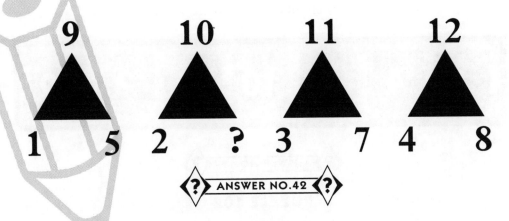

◇?◇ ANSWER NO.42 ◇?◇

PUZZLE 100

Zap the spaceship by finding a one-didgit number which will divide without remainder all the numbers which appear on it. Which number ought you to use?

LEVEL C

◇?◇ ANSWER NO.78 ◇?◇

PUZZLE 101

Here is a series of numbers.
Which number should replace the question mark?

| 1 | 4 | 7 | 10 | 13 | ? | 19 |

ANSWER NO.197

PUZZLE 102

How many 4s can be found in this stegosaurus?

FIENDISH FIGURES

ANSWER NO.162

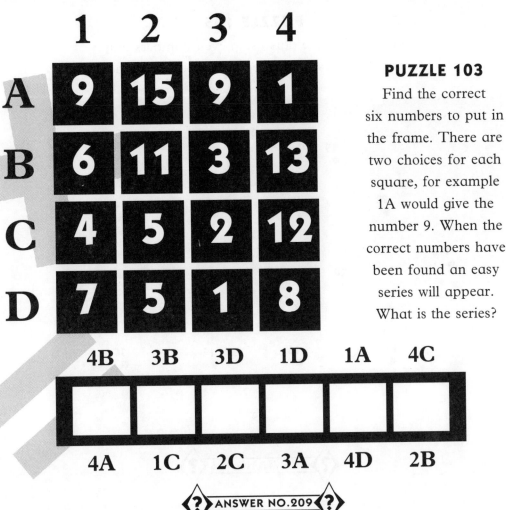

	1	2	3	4
A	9	15	9	1
B	6	11	3	13
C	4	5	2	12
D	7	5	1	8

PUZZLE 103

Find the correct six numbers to put in the frame. There are two choices for each square, for example 1A would give the number 9. When the correct numbers have been found an easy series will appear. What is the series?

4B	3B	3D	1D	1A	4C
4A	1C	2C	3A	4D	2B

◆ ? ▶ ANSWER NO.209 ◀ ? ◆

LEVEL C

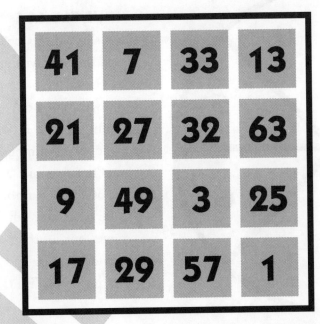

41	7	33	13
21	27	32	63
9	49	3	25
17	29	57	1

PUZZLE 104

Which of the numbers in the square is the odd one out and why?

◆ ? ▶ ANSWER NO.54 ◀ ? ◆

PUZZLE 105

Join together the dots using even numbers only.
Start at the lowest and discover the object. What is it?

ANSWER NO.126

PUZZLE 106

Each slice of this cake has a number written on it. Using the numbers shown how many different ways are there to add three numbers together to make a total of 13? A number can be used more than once, but a group cannot be repeated in a different order.

ANSWER NO.41

FIENDISH FIGURES

PUZZLE 107

Which of these pictures is not of the same box?

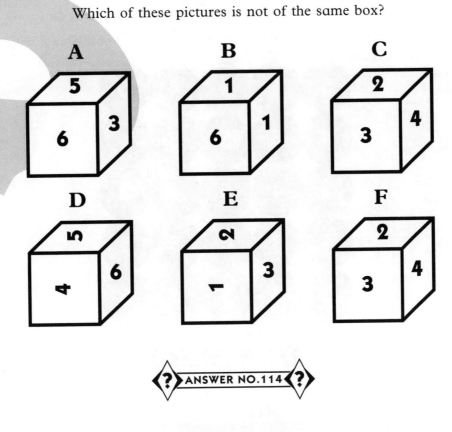

? ANSWER NO.114 ?

PUZZLE 108

Fill up this square with the numbers 1 to 5 so that no row, column
or diagonal line of five squares uses the same number more than once.
What number should replace the question mark?

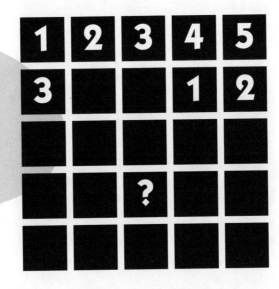

? ANSWER NO.219 ?

PUZZLE 109

Move up or across from the bottom left-hand 5 to the top right-hand 5.
Collect nine numbers and add them together. What is the highest you can score?

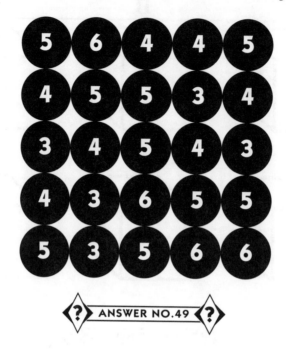

ANSWER NO.49

MIND NUMBING

★ LEVEL D ★

PUZZLE 110

The numbers in the middle section have some connection with those down the sides.
Find out what it is and tell us what should replace the question mark?

8	4	4
3	1	2
7	2	5
6	5	1
9	?	3

ANSWER NO.8

PUZZLE 111

Move up or across from the bottom left-hand 2 to the top right-hand 3.
Collect nine numbers and add them together. What is the highest you can score?

ANSWER NO.173

PUZZLE 112

Start at any corner and follow the lines. Add up the first four numbers you meet and then add on the corner number. What is the highest you can score?

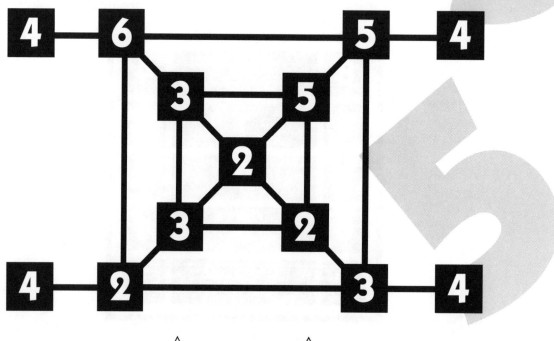

ANSWER NO.55

MIND NUMBING

PUZZLE 113

Place in the middle box a number larger than 1.
If the number is the correct one, all the other numbers can be divided
by it without leaving any remainder. What is the number?

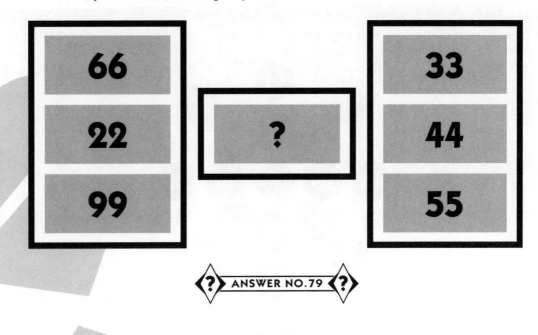

?> ANSWER NO.79 <?

PUZZLE 114

Each sector of the circle follows a pattern.
What number should replace the question mark?

?> ANSWER NO.151 <?

LEVEL D

PUZZLE 115

Here is an unusual safe. Each of the buttons must be pressed only once in the correct order to open it. The last button is marked F. The number of moves and the direction is marked on each button. Thus 1i would mean one move in, whilst 1O would mean one move out. 1C would mean one move clockwise and 1A would mean one move anti-clockwise.

Which button is the first you must press? Here's a clue: look around the outer rim.

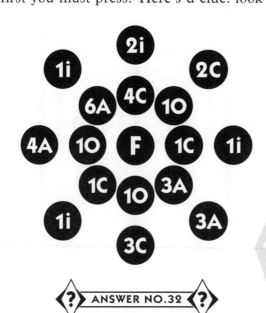

ANSWER NO.32

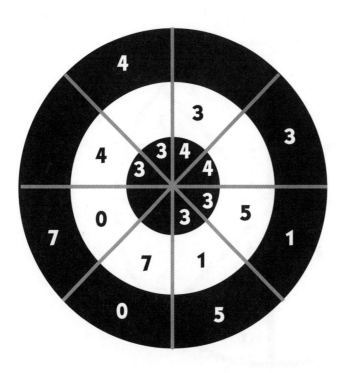

PUZZLE 116

Each slice of this cake adds up to the same number. Also each ring of the cake totals the same. Which number should appear in the blanks?

ANSWER NO.19

PUZZLE 117

Copy the cake slices out carefully and rearrange them to find the birthday.
How old was the birthday boy?

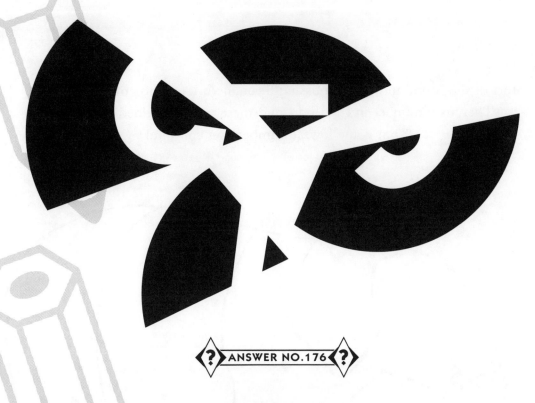

◆?▶ ANSWER NO.176 ◀?◆

PUZZLE 118

If you look carefully you should see why the numbers are written as they are.
What number should replace the question mark?

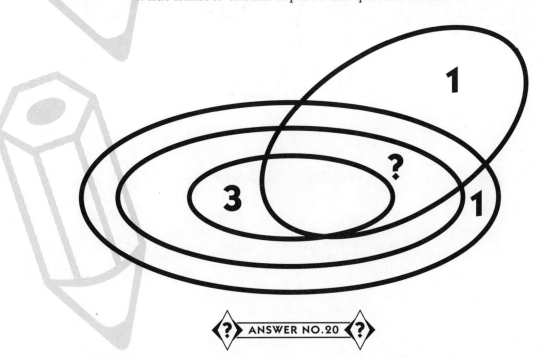

◆?▶ ANSWER NO.20 ◀?◆

LEVEL D

PUZZLE 119

Start at the A and move to B passing through various parts of the elephant.
There is a number in each part and these must be added together.
What is the lowest number you can total?

ANSWER NO.68

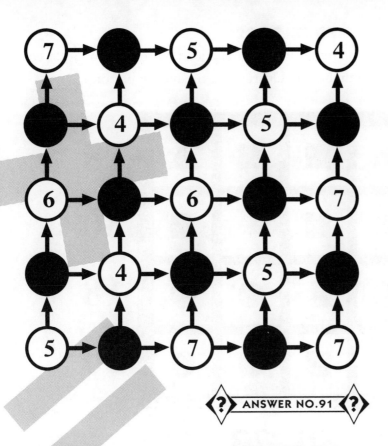

PUZZLE 120

Move from the bottom left-hand 5 to the top right-hand 4 adding together all five numbers. Each black circle is worth minus 3 and this should be taken away from your total each time you meet one. What is the highest total you can find?

ANSWER NO.91

PUZZLE 121

The numbers in column D are linked in some way to those in A, B and C. What number should replace the question mark?

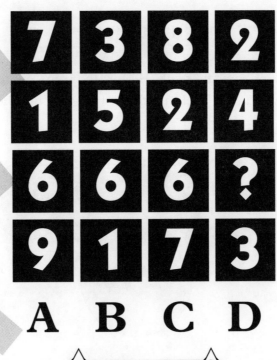

A B C D

ANSWER NO.139

PUZZLE 122

Each symbol is worth a number. The total of the symbols can be found alongside each row and column. What number should replace the question mark?

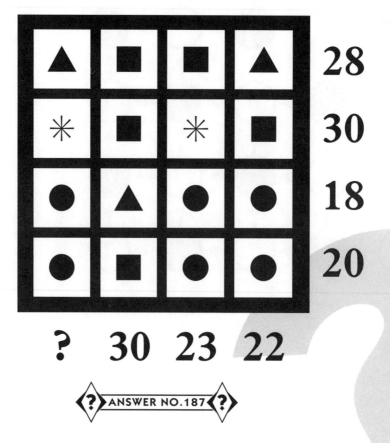

◇?◇ ANSWER NO.187 ◇?◇

PUZZLE 123

On the planet Venox the coins used are 1V, 2V, 5V, 10V, 20V and 50V. A Venoxian has 558V in his squiggly bank. He has the same number of four kinds of coin. How many of each are there and what are they?

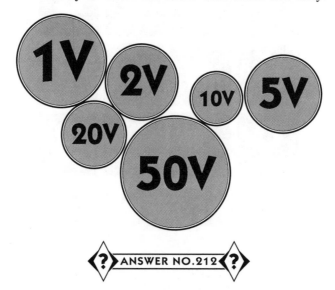

◇?◇ ANSWER NO.212 ◇?◇

PUZZLE 124

What is the lowest number of lines needed to divide the reindeer so that you can find the numbers 1, 2, 3, 4 and 5 in each section?

ANSWER NO.104

PUZZLE 125

Replace each question mark with either plus, minus, multiply or divide. Each sign can be used more than once. When the correct ones have been used the sum will be completed. What are the signs?

| 3 | ? | 4 | ? | 3 | ? | 8 | = | 7 |

ANSWER NO.103

PUZZLE 126

Follow the arrows and find the longest possible route.
How many boxes have been entered?

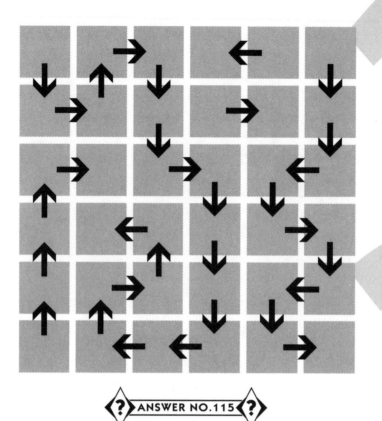

? ANSWER NO.115 ?

PUZZLE 127

The symbol on the flag will give a number. What is it?

? ANSWER NO.152 ?

MIND NUMBING

PUZZLE 128

Start at the middle 7 and move from circle to touching circle.
Collect three numbers and add them to the 7.
How many different routes are there to make a total of 20?

? ANSWER NO.31 **?**

PUZZLE 129

Divide up the box
into four identical
shapes. The numbers
in each shape add
up to the same.
How is this done?

? ANSWER NO.188 **?**

LEVEL D

PUZZLE 130

Scales 1 and 2 are in perfect balance. If one C is the same as four As, how many As are needed to balance the third set?

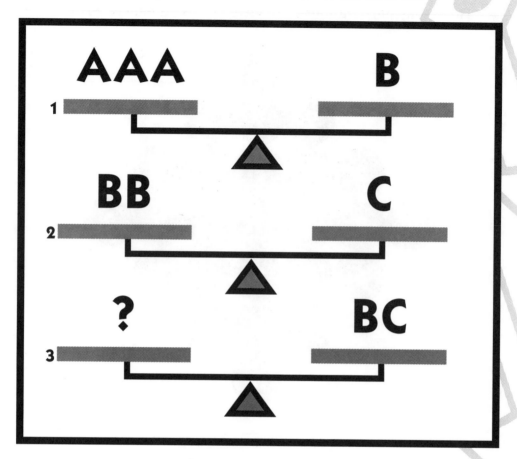

1 — AAA | B

2 — BB | C

3 — ? | BC

◆ **?** ANSWER NO.127 **?** ◆

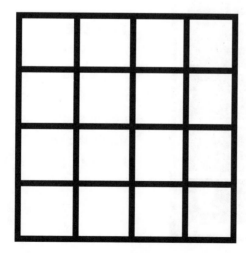

PUZZLE 131

How many rectangles of any size can you find in this diagram?

◆ **?** ANSWER NO.7 **?** ◆

MIND NUMBING

A B C D

	A	B	C	D
1	9 4 3	8 7 6	3 8 4	8 2 3
2	1 2 7	9 6 5	9 2 5	5 8 6
3	5 7 8	5 9 2	4 7 2	8 7 9
4	5 2 9	9 8 1	4 9 2	3 1 8

PUZZLE 132

Which squares contain the same numbers?

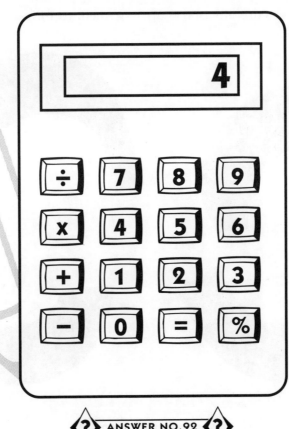

ANSWER NO.140

PUZZLE 133

Use either add, subtract, multiply or divide to give the number shown on the calculator. The same number must be used twice. what is the number?

ANSWER NO.92

LEVEL D

PUZZLE 134

Fill in the empty boxes so that every line adds up to 20.
What number should replace the question mark?

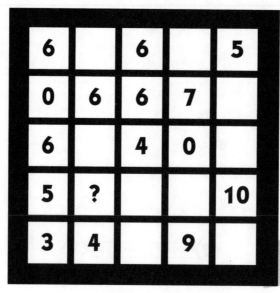

 ANSWER NO.67

PUZZLE 135

Copy out these shapes carefully and rearrange them to form a number. What is it?

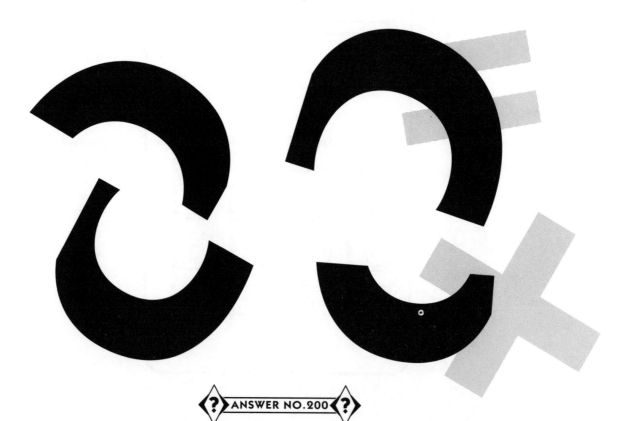

ANSWER NO.200

PUZZLE 136

Which number should replace the question mark to continue the series?

9   **15**   **21**   **27**

5   **7**   **11**   **13**   **?**   **19**   **23**   **25**

? ANSWER NO.44 ?

PUZZLE 137

The number 110 zaps this spaceship. Add together the numbers found on it and multiply the total by either 2, 3, 4, 5, 6, or 7. Which number ought you to use?

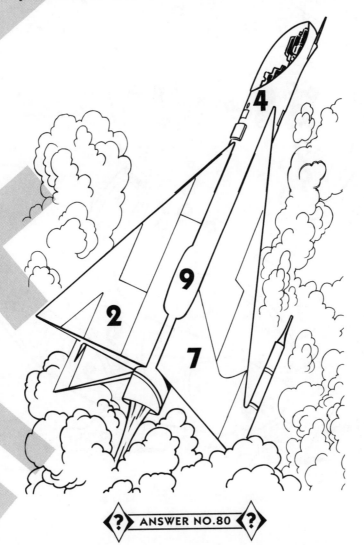

? ANSWER NO.80 ?

LEVEL D

PUZZLE 138

How many 9's can be found in this Tyrannosaurus Rex?

MIND NUMBING

ANSWER NO.164

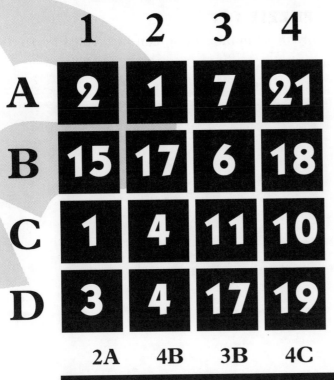

	1	2	3	4
A	2	1	7	21
B	15	17	6	18
C	1	4	11	10
D	3	4	17	19

PUZZLE 139

Find the correct six numbers to put in the frame. There are two choices for each square, for example 1A would give the number 2. When the correct numbers have been found an easy series will appear. What is the series?

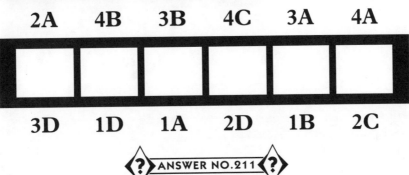

2A 4B 3B 4C 3A 4A

3D 1D 1A 2D 1B 2C

? ANSWER NO.211 ?

LEVEL D

16	28	14	44
24	52	48	8
40	4	64	36
12	32	56	20

PUZZLE 140

Which of the numbers in the square is the odd one out and why?

? ANSWER NO.56 ?

PUZZLE 141

Join together the dots using only those numbers that can be divided by 10.
Start at the lowest and discover the object. What is it?

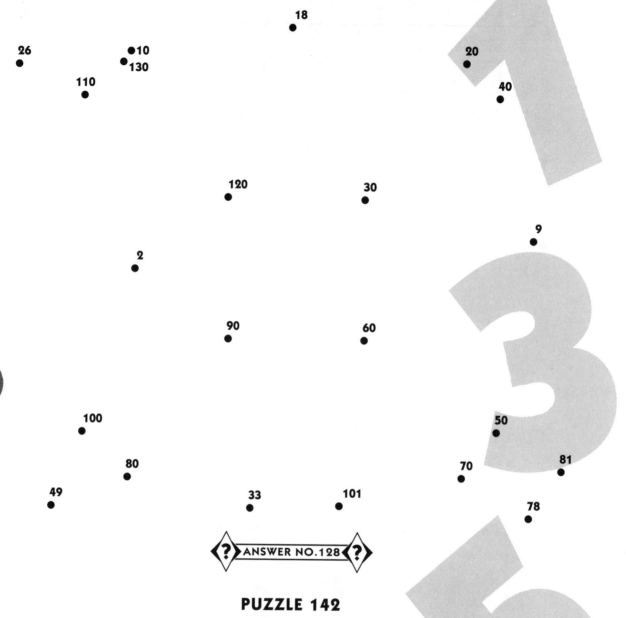

18

26

●10
130

110

20

40

120

30

9

2

90

60

D

100

50

80

70

81

49

33

101

78

◆? ANSWER NO.128 ?◆

PUZZLE 142

Here is a series of numbers.
Which number should replace the question mark?

| ? | 128 | 64 | 32 | 16 | 8 | 4 |

◆? ANSWER NO.199 ?◆

PUZZLE 143

Which of these pictures is not of the same box?

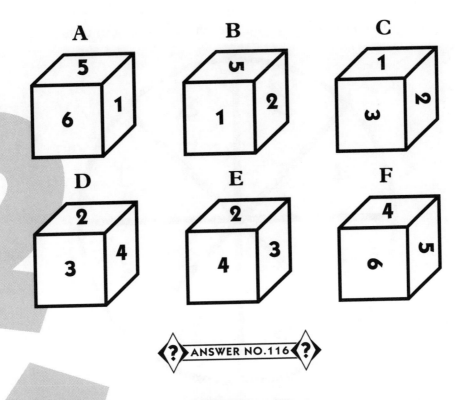

A   B   C
D   E   F

ANSWER NO.116

PUZZLE 144

Fill up this square with the numbers 1 to 5 so that no row, column or diagonal line of five squares uses the same number more than once. What number should replace the question mark?

ANSWER NO.74

PUZZLE 145

Each slice of this cake has a number written on it. Using the numbers shown how many different ways are there to add four numbers together to make a total of 12? A number can be used more than once, but a group cannot be repeated in a different order.

ANSWER NO.43

PUZZLE 146

Look at the pattern of numbers in the diagram.
What number should replace the question mark?

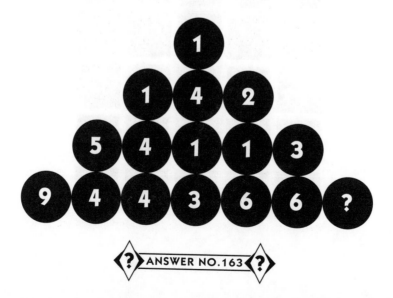

ANSWER NO.163

AAARGH!

PUZZLE 147

The numbers in the middle section have some connection with those down the sides.
Find out what it is and tell us what should replace the question mark?

8	2	4
6	3	2
9	3	3
7	7	1
4	?	2

 ANSWER NO.10

PUZZLE 148

Move up or across from the bottom left-hand 8 to the top right-hand 7.
Collect nine numbers and add them together. What is the lowest you can score?

?> ANSWER NO.177 <?

PUZZLE 149

Start at any corner and follow the lines. Add up the first four numbers you meet
and then add on the corner number. How many different routes will add up to 21?

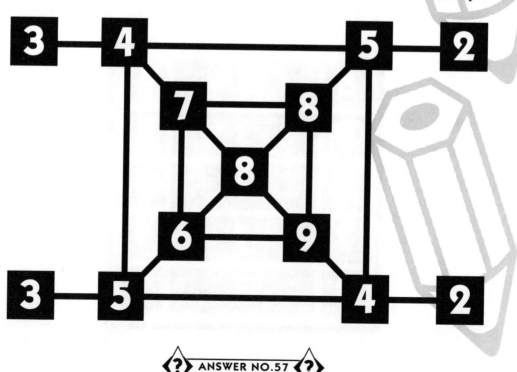

?> ANSWER NO.57 <?

AAARGH!

E

PUZZLE 150

Place in the middle box a number larger than 1.
If the number is the correct one, all the other numbers can be divided
by it without leaving any remainder. What is the number?

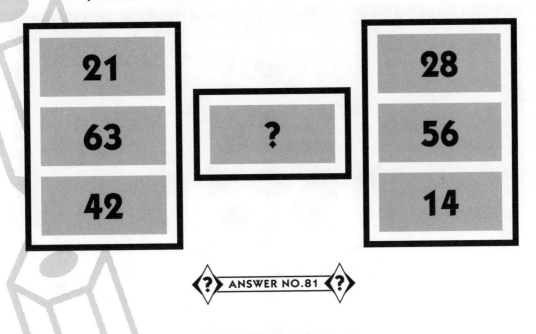

21		28
63	?	56
42		14

? ANSWER NO.81 ?

PUZZLE 151

Each sector of the circle follows a pattern.
What number should replace the question mark?

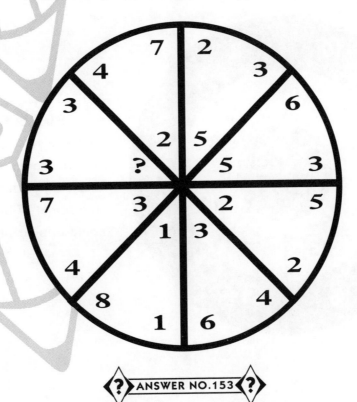

? ANSWER NO.153 ?

LEVEL E

PUZZLE 152

Here is an unusual safe. Each of the buttons must be pressed only once in the correct order to open it. The last button is marked F. The number of moves and the direction is marked on each button. Thus 1i would mean one move in, whilst 1O would mean one move out. 1C would mean one move clockwise and 1A would mean one move anti-clockwise.

Which button is the first you must press? Here's a clue: look on the inner circle.

ANSWER NO.34

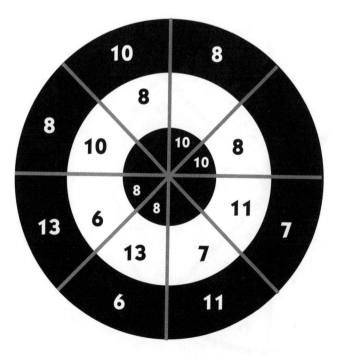

PUZZLE 153

Each slice of this cake adds up to the same number. Also each ring of the cake totals the same. Which number should appear in the blanks?

ANSWER NO.21

AAARGH!

E

PUZZLE 154

Copy the cake slices out carefully and rearrange them to find the birthday.
How old were the twins?

? ANSWER NO.178 ?

PUZZLE 155

If you look carefully you should see why the numbers are written as they are.
What number should replace the question mark?

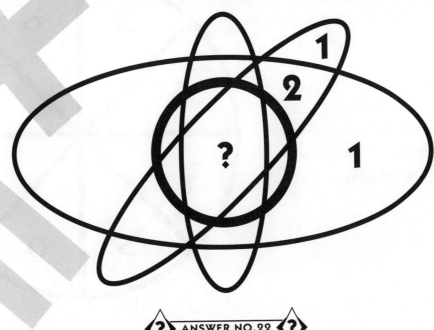

? ANSWER NO.22 ?

PUZZLE 156

Start at the A and move to B passing through various parts of the cow. There is a number in each part and these must be added together. What is the lowest number you can total?

ANSWER NO.70

PUZZLE 157

Each sector of this wheel has a number written on it. Using the numbers shown how many different ways are there to add four numbers together to make a total of 14? A number can be used more than once, but a group cannot be repeated in a different order.

ANSWER NO.45

AAARGH!

E

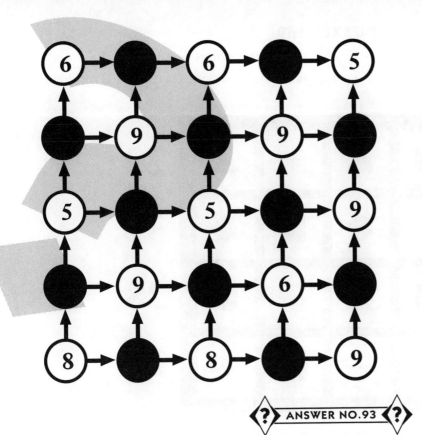

Move from the bottom
left-hand 8 to the top
right-hand 5 adding together
all five numbers. Each black
circle is worth minus 4 and this
should be taken away from
your total each time you meet
one. What is the lowest total
and how many different routes
are there to find it?

? ANSWER NO.93 **?**

PUZZLE 159

The numbers in column D are linked in some way to those in A, B and C.
What number should replace the question mark?

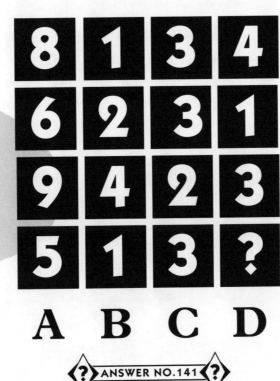

A B C D

? ANSWER NO.141 **?**

LEVEL E

PUZZLE 160

Each symbol is worth a number. The total of the symbols can be found alongside each row and column. What number should replace the question mark?

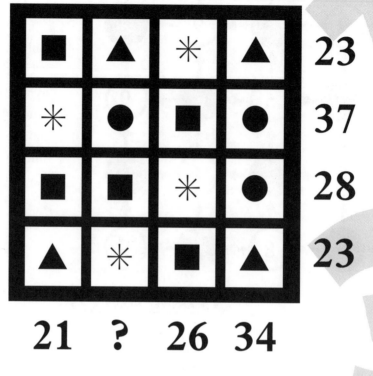

23
37
28
23

21 ? 26 34

‹?›ANSWER NO.189‹?›

PUZZLE 161

On the planet Venox the coins used are 1V, 2V, 5V, 10V, 20V and 50V. A Venoxian has 2,349V in his squiggly bank. He has the same number of five kinds of coin. How many of each are there and what are they?

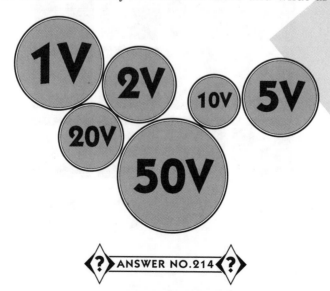

‹?›ANSWER NO.214‹?›

PUZZLE 162

What is the lowest number of lines needed to divide the bear so that
you can find the numbers 1, 2, 3, 4, 5 and 6 in each section?

◆?▶ANSWER NO.106 ◀?◆

PUZZLE 163

Replace each question mark with either plus, minus, multiply or divide.
Each sign can be used more than once. When the correct ones have been used
the sum will be completed. What are the signs?

4	?	5	?	3	?	8	=	24

◆?▶ANSWER NO.105 ◀?◆

PUZZLE 164

Follow the arrows and find the longest possible route.
How many boxes have been entered?

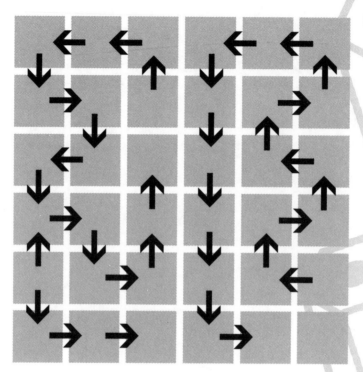

? ANSWER NO.117 **?**

PUZZLE 165

The symbol on the flag will give a number. What is it?

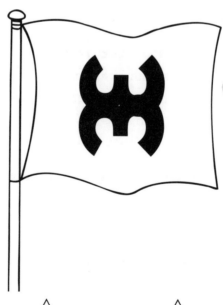

? ANSWER NO.154 **?**

AAARGH!

PUZZLE 166

Start at the middle 5 and move from circle to touching circle.
Collect three numbers and add them to the 5.
How many different routes are there to make a total of 16?

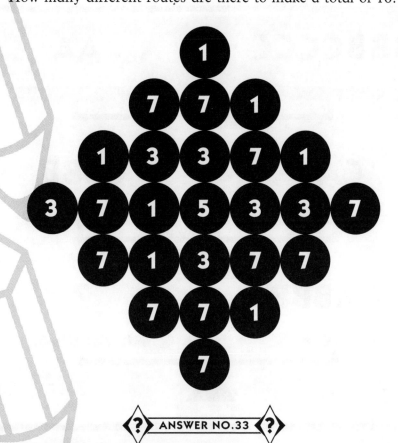

ANSWER NO.33

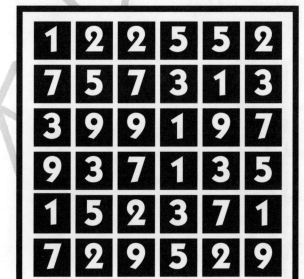

PUZZLE 167

Divide up the box
into six identical
shapes. The numbers
in each shape add
up to the same.
How is this done?

ANSWER NO.190

PUZZLE 168

Scales 1 and 2 are in perfect balance.
How many Cs are needed to balance the third set?

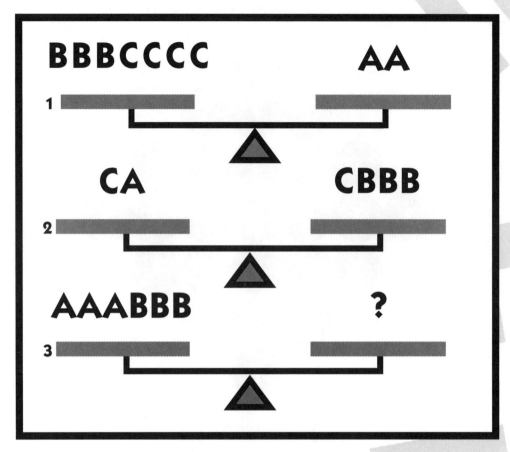

BBBCCCC   **AA**

1

CA   **CBBB**

2

AAABBB   **?**

3

ANSWER NO.129

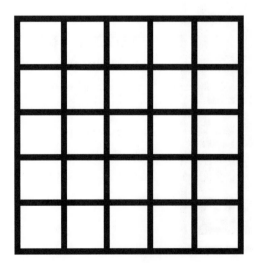

PUZZLE 169

How many squares
of any size can
you find in
this diagram?

ANSWER NO.9

A B C D E

	A	B	C	D	E
1	4 7 / 4 8	2 / 2 1	1 3 8 9	1 5 9 / 3	7 7 / 1 8
2	3 1 / 2	8 8 / 8	4 3 / 2 1	3 3 / 4 4	2 3 / 9 1
3	8 2 / 1 4	5 6 8 / 7	3 9 / 4 5	9 9 / 9 9	6 7 8 / 7
4	5 6 6 / 5	2 3 / 3 3	7 1 / 8 7	5 5 / 6 1	1 5 2 / 3
5	1 7 / 7 8	9 8 2 / 1	6 7 / 6 7	6 4 1 / 5	4 4 / 2 2

PUZZLE 170
Which squares contain the same numbers?

ANSWER NO.142

PUZZLE 171
What is the least number of buttons you must press to turn the number shown on the calculator into 17?

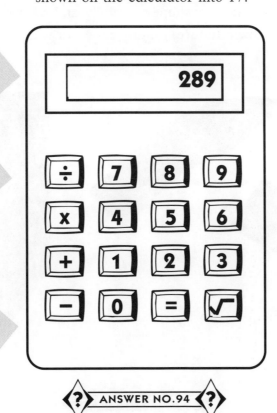

ANSWER NO.94

LEVEL E

3

PUZZLE 172

Fill in the empty boxes, using two numbers only, so that every line adds up to 25. What number should replace the question mark?

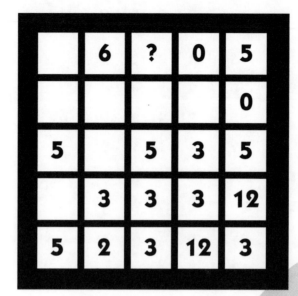

ANSWER NO.69

PUZZLE 173

Copy out these shapes carefully and rearrange them to form a number. What is it?

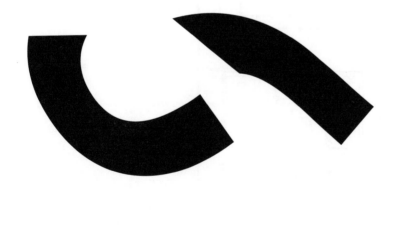

ANSWER NO.202

PUZZLE 174

Which number should replace the question mark to continue the series?

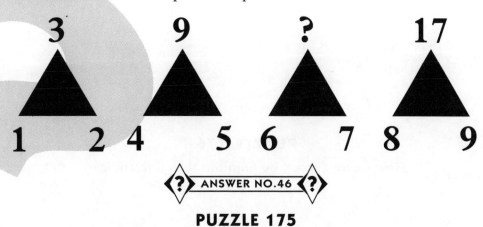

3   9   ?   17

1   2   4   5   6   7   8   9

<?> ANSWER NO.46 <?>

PUZZLE 175

To zap the spaceship find the number which, when multiplied by itself, will equal the total of the numbers shown. What is the number?

<?> ANSWER NO.84 <?>

LEVEL E

3

PUZZLE 176

How many 2's can be found in this Triceratops?

?⟩ ANSWER NO.166 ⟨?

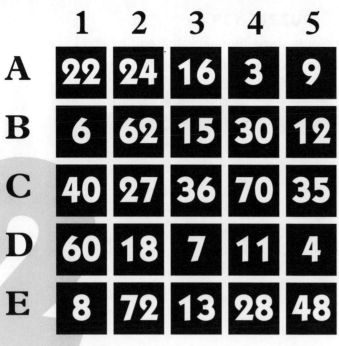

	1	2	3	4	5
A	22	24	16	3	9
B	6	62	15	30	12
C	40	27	36	70	35
D	60	18	7	11	4
E	8	72	13	28	48

PUZZLE 177

Find the correct six numbers to put in the frame. There are two choices for each square, for example 1A would give the number 22. When the correct numbers have been found a series will appear. What is the series?

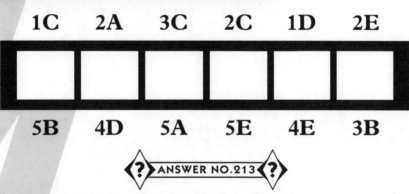

1C	2A	3C	2C	1D	2E
5B	4D	5A	5E	4E	3B

ANSWER NO.213

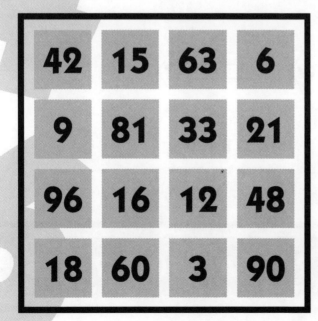

42	15	63	6
9	81	33	21
96	16	12	48
18	60	3	90

PUZZLE 178

Which of the numbers in the square is the odd one out and why?

ANSWER NO.58

LEVEL E

3

PUZZLE 179

Join together the dots using only those numbers that can be divided by 5.
Start at the lowest and discover the object. What is it?

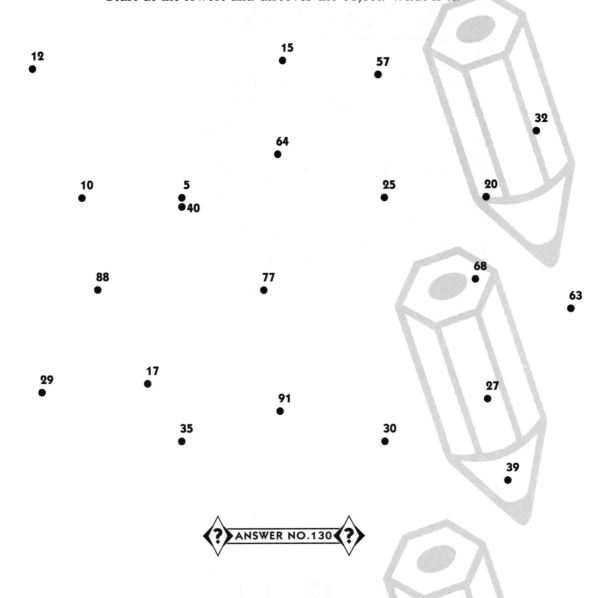

12

15

57

32

64

10

5

●40

25

20

68

63

88

77

29

17

27

91

35

30

39

◆?▷ANSWER NO.130◁?◆

PUZZLE 180

Here is a series of numbers.
Which number should replace the question mark?

| 32 | 25 | ? | 14 | 10 | 7 | 5 |

◆?▷ANSWER NO.201◁?◆

AAARGH!

PUZZLE 181

Which of these pictures is not of the same box?

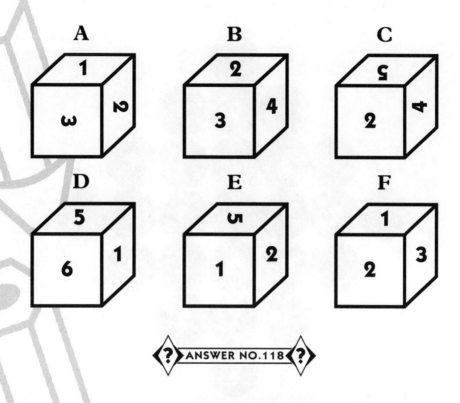

ANSWER NO.118

PUZZLE 182

Fill up this square with the numbers 1 to 5 so that no row, column or diagonal line of five squares uses the same number more than once. What number should replace the question mark?

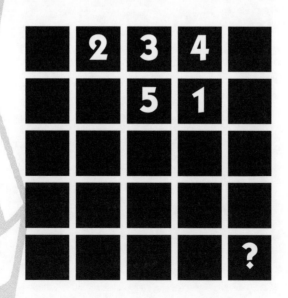

ANSWER NO.50

PUZZLE 183

Look at the pattern of numbers in the diagram.
What number should replace the question mark?

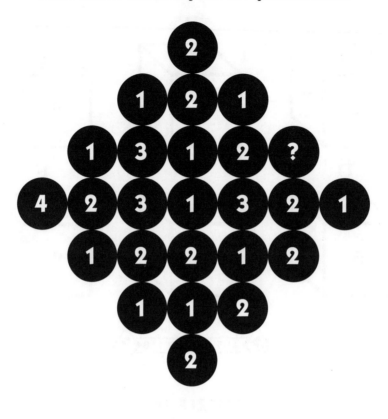

ANSWER 165

SUPER GENIUS

★ LEVEL F ★

PUZZLE 184

The numbers in the middle section have some connection with those down the sides.
Find out what it is and tell us what should replace the question mark?

3	51	5
8	46	8
2	41	7
3	21	4
6	?	9

ANSWER NO.12

PUZZLE 185

Move up or across from the bottom left-hand 5 to the top right-hand 3.
Collect nine numbers and add them together. What is the highest you can score?

 ANSWER NO.179

PUZZLE 186

Start at any corner and follow the lines. Add up the first four numbers you meet
and then add on the corner number. What is the lowest possible total
and how many different routes lead to it?

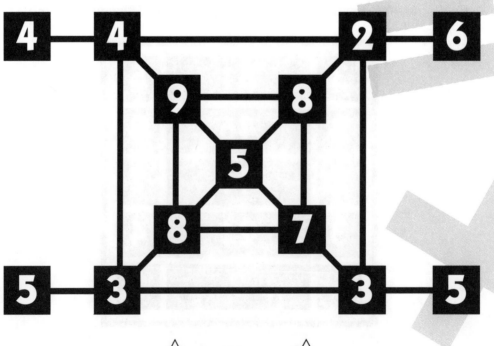

ANSWER NO.59

PUZZLE 187

Place in the middle box a number larger than 1.
If the number is the correct one, all the other numbers can be divided
by it without leaving any remainder. What is the number?

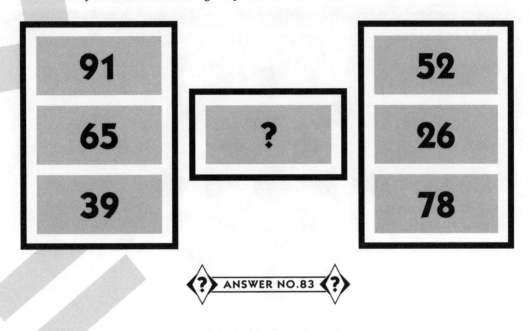

? ANSWER NO.83 ?

PUZZLE 188

Each sector of the circle follows a pattern.
What number should replace the question mark?

? ANSWER NO.155 ?

LEVEL F

F

PUZZLE 189

Here is an unusual safe. Each of the buttons must be pressed only once in the correct order to open it. The last button is marked F. The number of moves and the direction is marked on each button. Thus 1i would mean one move in, whilst 1O would mean one move out. 1C would mean one move clockwise and 1A would mean one move anti-clockwise. Which button is the first you must press? Here's a clue: look on the outer rim.

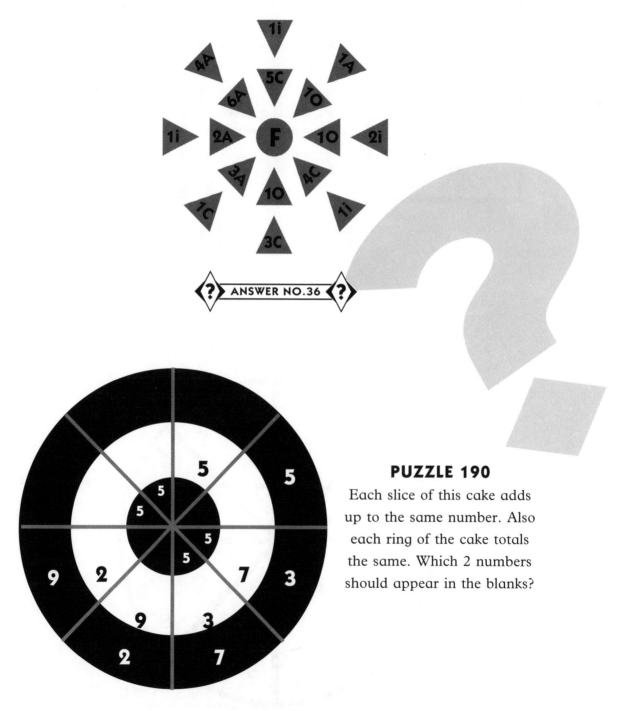

ANSWER NO.36

SUPER GENIUS
F

PUZZLE 190

Each slice of this cake adds up to the same number. Also each ring of the cake totals the same. Which 2 numbers should appear in the blanks?

ANSWER NO.23

PUZZLE 191

Copy the cake slices out carefully and rearrange them to find the birthday.
How old was the birthday girl?

<?>ANSWER NO.180<?>

PUZZLE 192

If you look carefully you should see why the numbers are written as they are.
What number should replace the question mark?

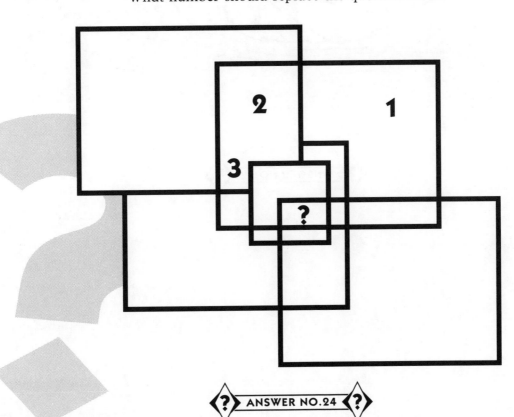

2

1

3

?

<?>ANSWER NO.24<?>

PUZZLE 193

Start at the A and move to B passing through the various parts of the duck.
There is a number in each part and these must be added together.
What is the lowest number you can total?

ANSWER NO.72

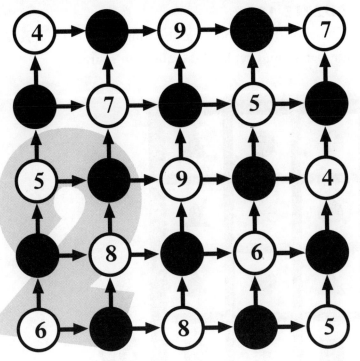

PUZZLE 194

Move from the bottom left-hand 6 to the top right-hand 7 adding together all five numbers. Each black circle is worth minus 5 and this should be taken away from your total each time you meet one. How many different routes, each giving a total of 10, can be found?

ANSWER NO.95

PUZZLE 195

The numbers in column D are linked in some way to those in A, B and C. What number should replace the question mark?

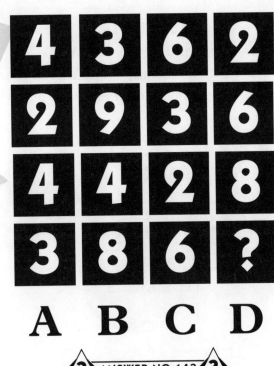

A   B   C   D

ANSWER NO.143

LEVEL F

PUZZLE 196

Each symbol is worth a number. The total of the symbols can be found alongside a row and two columns. What number should replace the question mark?

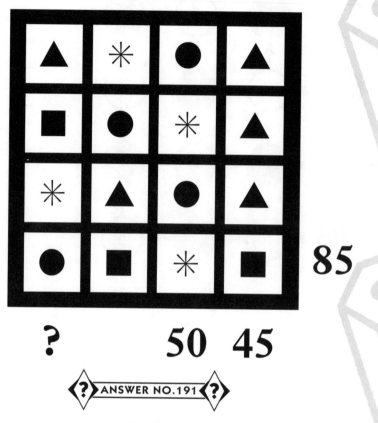

85

? 50 45

ANSWER NO.191

PUZZLE 197

On the planet Venox the coins used are 1V, 2V, 5V, 10V, 20V and 50V. A Venoxian has 3,071V in his squiggly bank. He has the same number of five kinds of coin. How many of each are there and what are they?

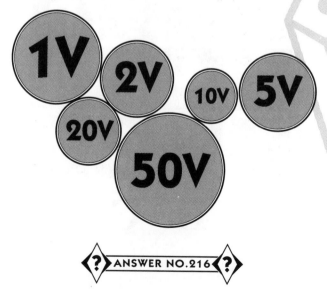

ANSWER NO.216

PUZZLE 198

What is the lowest number of lines needed to divide the cat so that
the numbers in each section always total 17?

? ANSWER NO.108 ?

PUZZLE 199

Replace each question mark with either plus, minus, multiply or divide.
Each sign can be used more than once. When the correct ones have been used
the sum will be completed. What are the signs?

| 10 | ? | 2 | ? | 7 | ? | 3 | = | 32 |

? ANSWER NO.107 ?

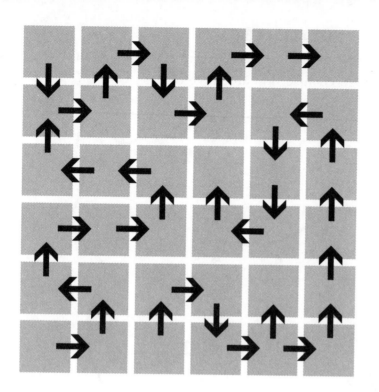

PUZZLE 200

Follow the arrows and find
the longest possible route.
How many boxes have
been entered?

?ANSWER NO.119?

PUZZLE 201

The symbol on the flag will give a number. What is it?

?ANSWER NO.156?

PUZZLE 202

Start at the middle 9 and move from circle to touching circle. Collect three numbers and add them to the 9. How many different routes are there to make a total of 17?

ANSWER NO.35

PUZZLE 203

Divide up the box into four identical shapes. The numbers in each shape add up to the same. How is this done?

ANSWER NO.192

LEVEL F

PUZZLE 204

Scales 1 and 2 are in perfect balance.
How many Bs are needed to balance the third set?

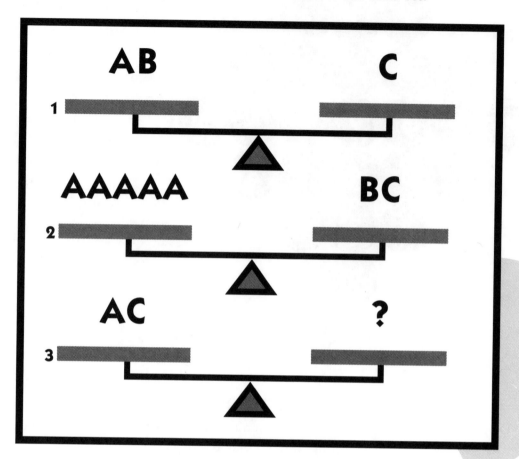

? ANSWER NO.131 ?

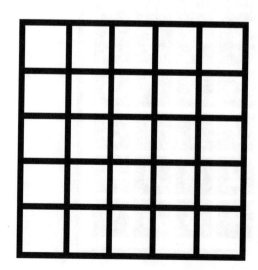

PUZZLE 205

How many rectangles
of any size can
you find in
this diagram?

? ANSWER NO.11 ?

PUZZLE 206

Which squares contain the same numbers?

	A	B	C	D	E
1	3 4 6 9	1 8 3 8	2 6 4 8	1 2 3 4	1 6 3 9
2	5 1 3 5	9 1 2 8	2 3 3 2	1 3 9 7	5 6 5 5
3	1 3 9 6	1 4 7 8	4 4 3 3	6 3 9 1	1 5 9 8
4	7 7 6 6	6 7 8 9	9 9 8 2	9 9 9 1	9 6 4 8
5	4 6 3 7	8 2 3 4	3 1 6 9	4 6 9	8 8 8 8

ANSWER NO.144

PUZZLE 207

How many ways are there to score 25 on this dartboard using four darts only? Each dart always lands in a segment and no dart falls to the floor. Once a group of numbers has been used it cannot be repeated in a different order.

ANSWER NO.47

LEVEL F

PUZZLE 208

Fill in the empty boxes so that every line adds up to 30. Use two numbers only, one of which is double the other. What number should replace the question mark?

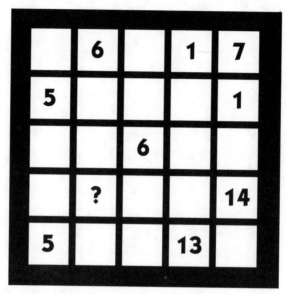

ANSWER NO.71

PUZZLE 209

Copy out these shapes carefully and rearrange them to form a number. What is it?

ANSWER NO.204

PUZZLE 210

Which number should replace the question mark to continue the series?

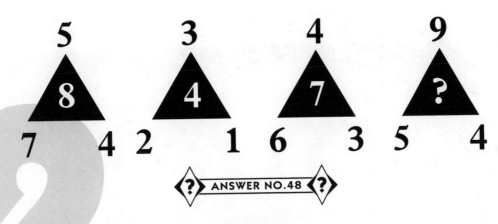

❓ ANSWER NO.48 ❓

PUZZLE 211

To zap the spaceship find the number which, when multiplied by itself, will equal the total of the numbers shown. What is the number?

❓ ANSWER NO.82 ❓

LEVEL F

PUZZLE 212

How many 8's can be found in this Brontosaurus?

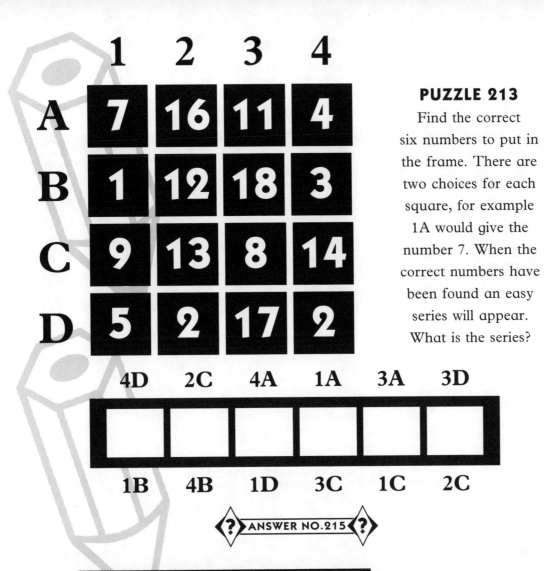

	1	2	3	4
A	7	16	11	4
B	1	12	18	3
C	9	13	8	14
D	5	2	17	2

PUZZLE 213

Find the correct six numbers to put in the frame. There are two choices for each square, for example 1A would give the number 7. When the correct numbers have been found an easy series will appear. What is the series?

4D	2C	4A	1A	3A	3D
1B	4B	1D	3C	1C	2C

ANSWER NO.215

LEVEL F

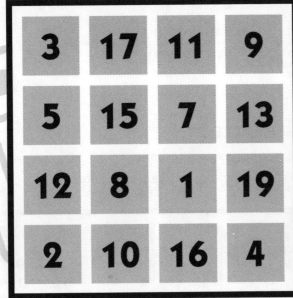

3	17	11	9
5	15	7	13
12	8	1	19
2	10	16	4

PUZZLE 214

Which two numbers on the square do not fit the pattern and why?

ANSWER NO.60

PUZZLE 215

Join together the dots using only those numbers that can be divided by 4.
Start at the lowest and discover the object. What is it?

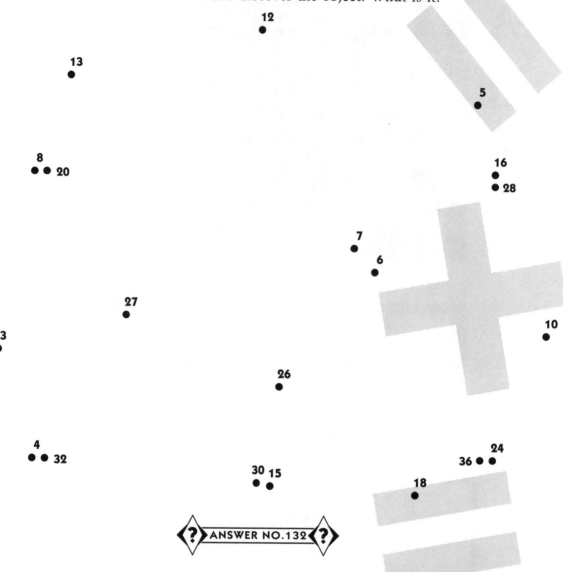

12
13
5
8
20
16
28
7
6
27
46 3
10
26
4 32
24
36
18
30 15

SUPER GENIUS

F

 ? ANSWER NO.132 ?

PUZZLE 216

Here is a series of numbers.
Which number should replace the question mark?

| 49 | 7 | 9 | 3 | 64 | 8 | 25 | ? |

? ANSWER NO.203 ?

PUZZLE 217

Which of these pictures are not of the same box?

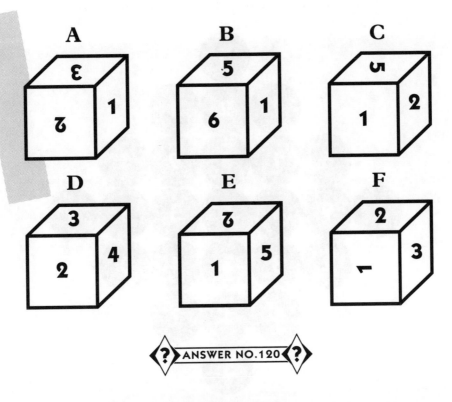

? ANSWER NO.120 **?**

PUZZLE 218

Fill up this square with the numbers 1 to 5 so that no row, column
or diagonal line of five squares uses the same number more than once.
What number should replace the question mark?

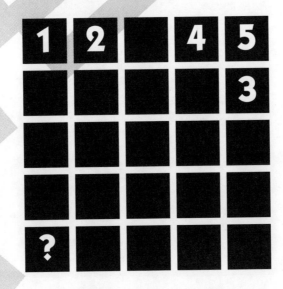

? ANSWER NO.96 **?**

PUZZLE 219

Look at the pattern of number in the diagram.
What number should replace the question mark?

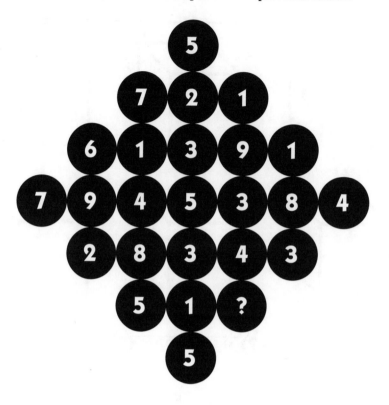

ANSWER NO.167

ANSWERS

1   14.

2   8. The numbers down the sides are placed together in the middle section.

3   30.

4   19. The numbers down the sides are placed together in the middle section in reverse order.

5   36.

6   11. The numbers down the sides are added together to give the number in the middle section.

7   100.

8   6. The number down the right-hand side is taken from the the number down the left-hand side to give the number in the middle section.

9   55.

10   2. The number down the left-hand side is divided by the number down the right-hand side to give the number in the middle section.

11   225.

12   45. The numbers down the sides are multiplied together to give the number in the middle section, placed in a reversed order.

13   3.

14   1. The number is surrounded by only one shape.

15   2 in the outer section and 4 in the inner one.

16   3. The number is found in 3 overlapping shapes.

17   8 in the outer section at the top, 3 in the outer section below and 5 in the inner one.

18   3. The number is found in 3 overlapping shapes.

19   2.

20   3. The number is found in 3 overlapping shapes.

21   9.

22   4. The number is found in 4 overlapping shapes.

23   4 and 6.

24   4. The number is found in 4 overlapping shapes.

25   4.

26   2D, in the third column.

27   7.

28   1R.

29   6.

30   2S, in the fourth column.

31   10.

32   1i, found between 4A and 3C.

33   13.

34   1C.

35   12.

36   1C.

37   9.

38   8.

39   8.

40   9.

41   8.

42   6. Move from triangle to triangle, beginning on the left, to read 1, 2, 3, 4. Start again to get 5, 6, 7, 8. Then move to the top to get 9, 10, 11, 12.

43   7.

44   17. Odd numbers increase in order from left, to right, to top around each triangle.

45   23.

46   13. The two numbers at the base of each triangle are added to give the top number.

47	22.
48	10. The left-hand number is added to the top number and then the right-hand number is subtracted to give the centre number.
49	42.
50	3.
51	14.
52	7. It is the only odd number.
53	23.
54	32. It is the only even number.
55	23.
56	14. All the other numbers are divisible by 4.
57	4.
58	16. All the other numbers are divisible by 3.
59	16 is the lowest and there are 2 routes.
60	Each pair of numbers on each row total 20. The first two on the bottom row, 2 and 10, do not.
61	1.
62	11.
63	2.
64	12.
65	0 and 6.
66	10.
67	1.
68	27.
69	7.
70	31.
71	4.
72	13.
73	2.
74	4.
75	3.
76	19.
77	5.
78	2.
79	11.
80	5.
81	7.
82	12.
83	13.
84	13.
85	19.
86	Times and 2.
87	30.
88	8, times and 8.

89	20.
90	12.
91	18.
92	2. 2 times 2 or 2 plus 2.
93	13 and one way.
94	1. Square root.($\sqrt{}$)
95	5.
96	3.
97	Plus and plus.
98	2.

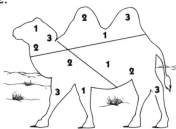

99	Plus and minus.
100	3.

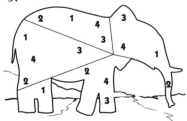

101	Minus, times and plus.
102	3.

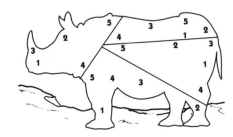

103	Multiply, plus and minus.
104	4.

105	Plus, divide and multiply.

106 4.

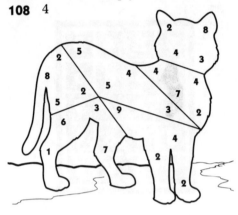

107 Divide, multiply and minus.
108 4

109 18.
110 C.
111 13.
112 F.
113 16.
114 B.
115 17.
116 E.
117 17.
118 F.
119 19.
120 D and E.
121 6.
122 A hammer.
123 2.
124 A tent.
125 6.
126 A Star.
127 9.
128 A Maltese Cross.
129 16.
130 An arrow.
131 2.
132 An envelope.
133 6. Add together A, B and C to get D.

134 1A and 3C.
135 9. Add together A, B and C in order to get D.
136 1B and 4D.
137 7. Add together A, B and C to get D.
138 3B and 1D.
139 6. Add together A and B, then take away C in order to get D.
140 2C, 3B and 4A.
141 1. A minus B minus C gives D.
142 1E, 4C and 5A.
143 4. A times B divided by C gives D.
144 1E, 3A, 3D and 5C.
145 3. Each sector contains the numbers 1, 2 and 3.
146 3. A 3 and its mirror image are placed together.
147 23. The numbers 1 to 24 are contained in the sectors.
148 7. A 7 and its mirror image are placed together.
149 2. The numbers in each sector total 12.
150 4. A 4 and its mirror image are placed together.
151 1. Each sector's total increases by 1.
152 2. A 2 and its mirror image are placed together top and bottom.
153 3. Opposite sectors total the same.
154 3. A 3, on its side, and its mirror image are placed together.
155 9. Each sector in the bottom half of the circle totals double its opposite.
156 5. A 5 and its mirror image are placed together.
157 1. The pattern is symmetrical.
158 10.
159 2. The pattern is symmetrical.
160 26.
161 4. The total of each horizontal line increases by 1.
162 30.
163 9. Each column of numbers totals 9.

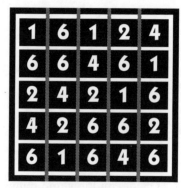

164 65.
165 1. The total of each horizontal line doubles from the outside to the centre.
166 40.
167 4. The total of each horizontal line doubles from the outside to the centre.
168 97.
169 12.
170 10.
171 15.
172 7.
173 41.
174 21.
175 15.
176 5.
177 50.
178 14.
179 47.
180 12.
181 8.
182

2	5	5	9
8	9	2	5
5	8	9	2
9	2	8	8

183 9.
184

7	3	3	7
6	4	6	4
3	6	3	7
4	7	6	4

185 22.

186

1	6	1	2	4
6	6	4	6	1
2	4	2	1	6
4	2	6	6	2
6	1	6	4	6

187 21.
188

9	8	4	3
3	5	8	5
4	4	3	9
3	5	8	4
9	8	9	5

189 30.
190

1	2	2	5	5	2
7	5	7	3	1	3
3	9	9	1	9	7
9	3	7	1	3	5
1	5	2	3	7	1
7	2	9	5	2	9

191 60.
192

2	9	5	5	1	6
4	8	1	9	5	2
7	3	6	2	7	8
6	3	7	1	7	3
1	8	2	8	3	4
9	5	4	4	6	9

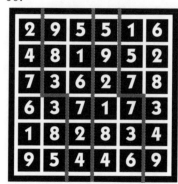

193 3. The series reads 1, 2, 3, 1, 2, 3, etc.

194 4.

195 28. The numbers increase by 4 each time.

196 3.

197 16. The numbers increase by 3 each time.

198 5.

199 256. The numbers halve from the left each time.

200 8.

201 19. The series of numbers decreases from the left by 7, then 6, then 5, then 4, etc.

202 2.

203 5. Each number has its square root placed next to it.

204 5.

205 1 2 3 4 5 6. The numbers increase by 1 each time.

206 5 of 2V, 5V and 10V coins.

207 2 4 6 8 10 12. The numbers increase by 2 each time.

208 22 of 2V, 5V and 10V coins.

209 1 3 5 7 9 11. The numbers increase by 2 each time.

210 17 of 1V, 2V, 5V and 10V coins.

211 1 3 6 10 15 21. The numbers increase by 2, 3, 4, etc.

212 31 of 1V, 2V, 5V and 10V coins.

213 12 24 36 48 60 72. The numbers increase by 12 each time.

214 27 of 2V, 5V, 10V, 20V and 50V coins.

215 2 3 5 7 11 13. These are all prime numbers.

216 37 of 1V, 2V, 10V, 20V and 50V coins.

217 5.

218 2.

219 4.